BEING A LEARNER

Siddharth Nimavat

INDIA · SINGAPORE · MALAYSIA

Dedicated to my lovely students and all the learners
around the world

Contents

Contents

Preface

As a teacher, I have always believed that education is far more than just a structured process of attending classes, passing examinations, and obtaining degrees. Education, to me, is the foundation upon which individuals build not only their careers but also their character, their worldview, and their sense of responsibility towards society. Yet, over the years, I have seen a troubling shift — a growing sense of disillusionment among students, teachers, and even parents.

One particular incident stands out vividly in my memory — an incident that ultimately inspired me to write this book. During break time, I overheard a group of students talking amongst themselves. One of them said, with frustration in his voice, "What's the point of all this studying? Even after completing degrees, people are sitting unemployed. This education is useless."

His words struck me deeply. Here was a young student, still in school, already disheartened by the very system meant to empower him. I knew this wasn't just the voice of one child — it was the reflection of a much larger crisis — a crisis of faith in our education system.

As a teacher, this shook me to the core. Education, something I had always cherished as the greatest tool for personal and societal growth, was being dismissed as a pointless ritual. That moment planted a seed in my mind — why are our students losing faith in education? Is the system failing to evolve with time? Are we preparing them only to pass exams, but not to face life?

This book is my humble attempt to address these very questions. Through these twelve chapters, I have explored what education truly means, how we can improve the quality of teaching and learning in our schools and colleges, and how we can go beyond textbooks to nurture ethical, emotional, and socially aware citizens. I have also examined the roles of teachers, parents, students, and society — because I firmly believe that education is not the responsibility of schools alone. It is a collective duty that belongs to every individual who dreams of a better future for our nation.

While writing this book, I drew heavily from my personal experiences in the classroom — the struggles of students trying to memorize concepts they don't understand, the frustration of parents who equate marks with success, and the helplessness of teachers who are caught between outdated syllabi and unrealistic expectations. But amidst all these challenges, I also saw hope — in the eyes of a curious child asking 'why', in the creative solutions some teachers bring into their classrooms, and in the silent but powerful resilience of parents who want a better life for their children.

This book is not meant to be an academic treatise or a policy document. It is, instead, a conversation — between a teacher and society, between a citizen and the system, between a dreamer and reality. It does not claim to have all the answers, but it aims to spark the right questions — questions we must all ask if we truly want to rebuild our education system.

I hope that every teacher, parent, student, and citizen who reads this book finds something to reflect upon. More than that, I hope it inspires each reader to see education not as a distant institution, but as a living, breathing process that shapes our families, communities, and future.

Together, we can rebuild the faith in education.

With sincerity and hope,

– Siddharth
Teacher & Lifelong Learner

INTRODUCTION

What is Education?

"Education is not the learning of facts, but the training of the mind to think."

– Albert Einstein

We have all grown up hearing that education is important. But what does it truly mean to be educated? Is it about securing good marks? Getting a degree? Or is it about learning something that changes the way we think and live?

Imagine a child who is full of curiosity—asking questions about the world, experimenting with new ideas, and exploring different ways to solve problems. Now imagine the same child, years later, memorizing textbooks, preparing for exams, and feeling pressure to score high marks. Somewhere along the way, the joy of learning often fades.

Education is not just about collecting information; it is about understanding, questioning, and applying knowledge to real life. It is about evolving with time, learning from experiences, and continuously growing as individuals and as a society.

In India, education has always been valued. From ancient learning centers like Takshashila and Nalanda to modern universities, we have a deep history of knowledge and wisdom. But today, we face many challenges—rote learning, outdated teaching methods, lack of practical exposure, and exam stress. How can we make learning more meaningful? How can we help students become thinkers, problem-solvers, and innovators rather than just memorizing facts?

This book, Being a Learner, is a journey to explore how we can improve education—not just in schools and colleges but in everyday life. We will discuss the roles of students, teachers, and parents in shaping a better learning culture. We will look at the challenges faced by students today and how we can overcome them. We will also explore emotional intelligence, life skills, and moral education—topics that are essential but often overlooked in traditional education.

Our approach in this book is not about blaming the system but about finding solutions. Education is evolving, and we have the power to shape its future. Whether you are a student, a teacher, or a parent, this book will help you rethink the way we learn and how we can make education better for ourselves and future generations.

So, let's start this journey together—let's not just study, but truly learn.

CHAPTER 1

Education Today: And Its Purpose

"The purpose of education is to replace an empty mind with an open one."

– Malcolm Forbes

Education is often seen as a path to success. But what exactly does it mean to be educated? Does it mean memorizing facts, passing exams, and earning degrees? Or does it mean developing the ability to think critically, solve problems, and adapt to a changing world?

Many of us have been taught to equate education with good grades. From an early age, we are encouraged to focus on marks, ranks, and degrees. Schools prepare us for exams, colleges prepare us for jobs, and somewhere in between, the actual essence of learning is lost.

Think about this—if a student memorizes the entire science textbook and scores full marks in an exam, does that mean they truly understand science? Do they know how to apply it to real-world problems? Can they think like a scientist, ask questions, and find answers? Or have they just memorized the words without grasping the meaning?

Why Has Education Become Exam-Centric?

The emphasis on exams has shaped the way students, parents, and teachers approach education. Exams are often seen as the ultimate test of knowledge. But do they really measure how much a student has learned? Or do they simply test how well a student can memorize and recall information under pressure?

In many schools, students spend months preparing for exams. Coaching classes, extra tuition, and late-night study sessions become routine. The goal is simple—score high marks. But what happens once the exams are over? A large percentage of students forget most of what they studied. If knowledge disappears after an exam, can we say real learning has happened?

This system affects not just students but also teachers. Many teachers feel pressured to complete the syllabus on time, leaving little room for creative teaching methods. Instead of encouraging curiosity and discussion, classrooms often become spaces where students passively listen and take notes.

Let's consider the story of two students, Ramesh and Amit.

Both are in the same class, studying the same subjects. Ramesh is an excellent student by traditional standards—he memorizes textbooks, scores high marks, and is praised for his discipline. Amit, on the other hand, struggles with rote memorization but is deeply curious. He often asks questions, tries to understand concepts, and enjoys applying what he learns to real-life situations.

One day, their teacher gives them an assignment on water conservation. Ramesh copies information from books and presents a detailed report filled with facts and statistics. Amit, however, visits a local village facing water shortages. He talks to the people there, observes the problem firsthand, and comes up with ideas on how to conserve water in a practical way.

When results are announced, Ramesh scores higher marks because his report was structured well and followed the textbook format. Amit, despite his unique approach, gets average marks. But years later, when faced with a real-life challenge, who do you think will be better equipped to find solutions?

This simple story highlights the gap between theoretical knowledge and real learning. If we want education to be meaningful, we must shift our focus from memorization to understanding and application.

The Shift from Curiosity to Compliance

When we observe young children, we notice something remarkable—they are naturally curious. A toddler asks endless 'why' questions, explores objects with fascination, and tries to understand the world through experimentation. This curiosity is the foundation of true learning.

But as children grow older and enter school, something changes. Learning, which was once about discovery, slowly turns into a structured routine. The same child who was once full of questions starts memorizing answers from textbooks. The joy of learning is replaced by the pressure of scoring high marks.

Why does this happen? Schools often reward obedience over originality. Students are taught to follow instructions, repeat information, and give 'correct' answers rather than think critically. The result? Many students stop questioning, stop exploring, and simply do what is expected of them.

This transition from curiosity to compliance is one of the biggest challenges in education today. But the good news is that we can change it. Schools, teachers, and parents can create environments where questioning is encouraged, mistakes are seen as learning opportunities, and creativity is nurtured rather than suppressed.

Lessons from the Past: How Ancient Education Was Different

Education has existed in various forms for centuries. If we look back at ancient Indian education, we find a very different approach compared to today's system. Gurukuls, the traditional Indian learning centers, focused on holistic development. Students lived with their teachers, learned through discussions, practical experiences, and storytelling.

Here's how Ancient Indian Education compared to Modern Education:

Aspect	Ancient Education (Gurukul System)	Modern Education
Learning Method	Practical, hands-on learning, discussions	Rote memorization, textbooks
Subjects Taught	Philosophy, ethics, astronomy, mathematics, warfare, medicine, and arts	Mainly academic subjects with limited life skills
Teacher-Student Relationship	Close bond; students lived with teachers (Guru-Shishya tradition)	Limited interaction beyond the classroom

What Can We Learn from the Best Education Systems in the World?

Globally, different countries have adopted unique approaches to education, and some have been more successful than others.

Case Study: Finland's Education Model

Finland is frequently ranked as having one of the best education systems in the world. But what makes it special?

1. No Standardized Exams: Instead of pressuring students with exams, Finland focuses on continuous learning and understanding.
2. Practical Learning: Schools emphasize problem-solving, creativity, and critical thinking over rote memorization.

3. Equal Opportunities: Every student, regardless of background, gets the same high-quality education.
4. Well-Trained Teachers: Teachers undergo extensive training and are given freedom to innovate in classrooms.

Imagine if we could bring some of these changes into our education system. Could we reduce exam stress? Could we make learning more engaging and meaningful?

The Boy Who Loved to Build

Arjun, a 12-year-old student, struggled with memorizing science concepts in school. He would often score low marks in exams, and teachers labeled him as 'weak.' However, at home, Arjun spent hours building small machines from scrap materials—he built a windmill using plastic bottles and a solar-powered lamp using spare wires.

One day, during a science competition, he presented a working model of a self-powered water purifier. The judges were amazed. A boy who was considered weak in science applied the very concepts he failed in exams to solve a real-world problem.

This raises an important question—Are exams the right way to measure intelligence and creativity?

A 2018 study by the National Center for Education Statistics (NCES) in the United States found that students learn best when they are actively engaged in the learning process rather than passively memorizing facts.

The study identified three key elements that improve learning:

1. Active Participation: Students learn better when they participate in discussions, experiments, or real-world applications.
2. Interdisciplinary Learning: Combining subjects (for example, using history to explain science) makes learning more interesting.
3. Personalized Learning: Every student has different strengths, and teaching methods should adapt to individual needs.

Looking Ahead: The Need for Change

Education should not be about memorizing facts just to pass exams. It should be about understanding concepts, applying knowledge, and thinking critically. Countries like Finland, Singapore, and Japan have transformed their education systems by focusing on these aspects.

Can India do the same? Absolutely! By making small changes—encouraging curiosity, promoting practical learning, and reducing exam pressure—we can make education more meaningful.

The Power of Learning from Experience

Some of the greatest minds in history—Leonardo da Vinci, Thomas Edison, Albert Einstein—did not rely solely on formal education. They were lifelong learners who asked questions, experimented, and learned through experience.

Einstein once said, 'I have no special talent. I am only passionately curious.'

This curiosity is what makes learning truly powerful. It allows us to grow beyond textbooks and classrooms and apply knowledge to real life.

How Can We Encourage True Learning?

1. Ask More Questions: Learning begins when we ask 'why,' 'how,' and 'what if?' instead of just memorizing answers.
2. Think Beyond the Syllabus: Knowledge is not limited to textbooks. Real learning happens when we explore beyond the syllabus.
3. Learn by Doing: The best way to understand something is to experience it—through experiments, observations, and practical applications.
4. Reflect on What We Learn: Instead of just reading or listening, taking time to reflect on how knowledge applies to life helps deepen understanding.

A Vision for the Future of Learning

True education should not be about filling minds with information, but about helping minds grow, question, and create.

If we focus on learning as an experience rather than just a requirement, we will not only become better students—we will become better thinkers, problem-solvers, and innovators.

The Psychology of Learning: How Our Minds Absorb Knowledge

Why do some students grasp new concepts quickly while others struggle? Why do we remember certain lessons for life while forgetting others almost immediately? The answer lies in the psychology of learning—understanding how our minds process, store, and retrieve information.

Psychologists have studied learning for decades and have identified several key factors that influence how we absorb and retain knowledge. Learning is not just about reading or listening—it involves cognitive processes, emotions, motivation, and even social interactions.

Understanding how the brain learns can help us optimize the way we study, teach, and apply knowledge.

The Science Behind Learning: How Our Brain Works

Type of Memory	How It Works	Example
Sensory Memory	Holds information for a few seconds before deciding what's important.	Seeing a math problem on the board but forgetting it immediately.

Type of Memory	How It Works	Example
Short-Term Memory	Holds information temporarily, but can be lost if not reinforced.	Remembering a phone number for a few minutes.
Long-Term Memory	Stores information permanently when repeated and applied.	Knowing how to ride a bicycle even after years.

How Psychology Helps in Learning More Effectively

Active Learning: Instead of passively reading, students learn better when they actively engage with the content. Discussing lessons with classmates, teaching concepts to others, or applying knowledge in practical situations makes it easier to retain information. Studies have shown that when students actively participate, they remember concepts for a longer period and develop a deeper understanding.

Spaced Repetition: Many students make the mistake of cramming all their study material in one go. However, research suggests that revisiting information at intervals strengthens memory. Revising a concept after a few days instead of studying it once and forgetting it helps move information from short-term to long-term memory.

Interleaving Learning: Studying one subject continuously can sometimes lead to boredom and reduced efficiency. A better approach is to mix different topics, which forces the brain to make connections between them.

For example, instead of spending hours on math alone, switching between math and science helps improve overall comprehension.

Self-Testing: Testing oneself with questions, quizzes, or flashcards is one of the most effective ways to strengthen memory. When students recall information rather than just reading it repeatedly, their brain works harder to retrieve knowledge, making it easier to remember later.

Using Mnemonics: Associating information with visual images, acronyms, or stories makes learning fun and memorable. For example, using 'VIBGYOR' to remember the colors of the rainbow helps retain information effortlessly. Mnemonics are especially useful in subjects like science, history, and language learning.

How Emotions Affect Learning

Motivation plays a crucial role in learning. When students find a subject interesting, they learn faster. Teachers and educators can enhance learning by making lessons interactive, relatable, and connected to real-life applications. If a student understands why a subject is important, they are more likely to stay engaged and curious.

Stress and Fear can negatively impact learning. Fear of failure, exam pressure, or a strict learning environment can cause students to freeze rather than focus. High anxiety levels interfere with memory recall, making it harder for students to perform well. Reducing stress through proper guidance, encouragement, and a supportive environment can enhance learning.

Curiosity and Exploration boost learning. When students are encouraged to ask questions and explore topics on their own, their brains become more engaged in problem-solving. Encouraging creativity, hands-on experiments, and open-ended questions helps students learn more effectively than just memorizing textbooks.

The Student Who Overcame Fear

A student, Rohan, was always nervous during math class. He believed he was 'bad at math' and avoided solving problems. However, his new teacher introduced a different approach—instead of focusing on getting the right answer, she encouraged students to explore different methods of solving problems.

By shifting the focus from marks to understanding, Rohan slowly started enjoying math. His fear turned into curiosity, and over time, his performance improved significantly.

This shows that when students feel safe, motivated, and curious, learning becomes much easier.

Applying the Psychology of Learning to Education

Encouraging discussions and exploration rather than just giving answers helps students engage more deeply with knowledge. When students are allowed to think critically, experiment, and express their ideas, they remember concepts better than when simply given predefined answers.

Making learning interactive through storytelling, problem-solving, and real-world applications creates a deeper understanding. Instead of relying solely on textbooks, integrating learning with everyday situations helps make education more meaningful.

Helping students overcome learning anxiety by shifting focus from grades to understanding is essential for effective education. If students are given the freedom to explore and make mistakes without the fear of punishment, they are more likely to develop confidence in their abilities.

By applying the psychology of learning, we can make education more effective, enjoyable, and meaningful for every student.

What Have We Discovered About True Learning?

As we reach the end of this chapter, let's take a moment to reflect on what we have explored so far.

We began by questioning what it truly means to learn. Is education just about memorizing facts and passing exams, or is it about curiosity, understanding, and real-world application? We discovered that while traditional education often focuses on grades, true learning is about making meaningful connections, asking the right questions, and applying knowledge in real life.

We also examined how the ancient education system focused on holistic learning, emphasizing values, skills, and real-world problem-solving. In contrast, modern education often prioritizes results over understanding. However, by adopting the best global practices, such as Finland's interactive and student-centered approach, we can transform the way we learn.

Next, we delved into the psychology of learning—understanding how our brain processes and retains knowledge. We learned that techniques like active learning, spaced repetition, interleaving subjects, and self-testing can significantly enhance how effectively we absorb information. Moreover, emotions and mindset play a vital role in learning. A positive, curious, and motivated mindset leads to better retention and deeper understanding.

How Does This Help Us Grow?

When we learn with curiosity rather than pressure, we unlock our full potential.

- If students apply psychological learning techniques, they will retain knowledge better and feel less overwhelmed by exams.
- If teachers focus on interactive and experience-based teaching, they will create a more engaging and effective learning environment.
- If we, as a society, shift our perspective from grades to growth, we will develop critical thinkers, innovators, and lifelong learners rather than just exam-takers.

A Thought for the Journey Ahead

Learning is not a destination; it is a journey.
The more we explore, question, and apply
knowledge, the more we grow. Education should
empower us—not just with information, but
with the ability to think, create, and adapt.

In the upcoming chapters, we will dive deeper into how we can reshape schools, colleges, and the education system to support true learning. We will also explore the roles of teachers, students, and parents in this journey of transformation.

As Albert Einstein once said:

"Education is what remains after one has forgotten what one has learned in school."

True learning stays with us forever, shaping who we are and what we become. Let's continue this journey with an open mind and a thirst for knowledge.

CHAPTER 2

Rethinking Schools – A Place for Exploration, Not Just Exams

Schools are often seen as the foundation of education, shaping young minds and preparing them for the future. But are our schools truly fostering a love for learning? Or have they become places where students memorize information, pass exams, and move to the next grade without truly understanding what they are learning?

The traditional schooling system, for many, feels like a race for marks rather than an environment for intellectual growth. Should schools only focus on exams, or should they be spaces where students explore, create, and develop essential life skills?

Education, as I have mentioned in the previous chapter, is not just about knowing facts but about understanding and applying them. Yet, most schools today still follow methods that emphasize memorization over creativity, structure over curiosity, and results over understanding.

Imagine two schools with very different approaches:

In **School A**, students sit quietly in rows, listening to their teacher explain a topic from a textbook. The focus is on completing the syllabus and preparing for exams. Students memorize information but rarely discuss or question what they are learning.

In **School B**, students work in groups, discuss ideas, and explore subjects through activities and real-world applications. The teacher encourages them to ask questions, think critically, and experiment with different learning methods.

Which school do you think produces students who love learning?

Unfortunately, many schools still function like School A, where learning is limited to textbooks and examinations. However, the future demands individuals who can think creatively, solve problems, and adapt to new challenges—something that traditional schooling does not always encourage.

Why Memorization Alone is Not Enough

Memorization has its place in learning, but when education is based solely on memorization, students struggle to apply their knowledge in real life.

For example, a student who memorizes mathematical formulas may score high in an exam but may not understand how to use them in practical situations. On the other hand, a student who learns by solving real-life problems develops a deeper understanding of concepts and gains the ability to apply knowledge in meaningful ways.

This is why schools should focus on exploration, critical thinking, and creativity instead of just exam scores.

How Can We Make Schools More Engaging?

Many successful education systems around the world focus on learning by doing rather than just memorizing textbooks. Schools should:

- Encourage interactive and discussion-based learning instead of passive listening.
- Provide real-world applications of concepts so that students understand why they are learning something.
- Introduce projects and activities that promote problem-solving and creativity.

A classroom should be a place of curiosity and engagement, not just silent note-taking. When students actively participate in their learning, they remember concepts better, develop problem-solving skills, and build confidence.

However, in many traditional classrooms, the method of teaching remains one-directional—the teacher speaks, and the students listen. This creates a passive learning environment, where students receive information without questioning or analyzing it. Research shows that students learn best when they are encouraged to think, ask questions, and apply their knowledge in real situations.

The Power of Inquiry-Based Learning

What happens when students take charge of their learning? Inquiry-based learning allows students to explore topics through curiosity and investigation rather than just memorizing textbook content.

For example, instead of a teacher saying, 'Photosynthesis is the process by which plants make food using sunlight,' an inquiry-based lesson would begin with:

'Why do you think plants grow towards the sunlight? What would happen if a plant is kept in the dark?'

By making students think, question, and experiment, they develop a deeper understanding of concepts rather than just memorizing facts.

A Story: The Science Class That Changed Everything

A group of students dreaded their weekly science class because they found it boring and difficult. Their teacher, Mr. Rao, decided to change the way he taught. Instead of lecturing from a textbook, he transformed the classroom into a science lab.

He asked his students to grow plants under different conditions—one in sunlight, one in the dark, and one with artificial light. Over weeks, the students observed, recorded data, and discussed their findings. By the end of the experiment, not only had they understood photosynthesis, but they also enjoyed the process of learning.

This method of learning by doing is far more effective than simply memorizing a definition.

How Technology Can Make Learning More Engaging

Technology, when used correctly, can make learning interactive and exciting. Instead of being passive listeners, students can use digital tools to visualize concepts, experiment with virtual labs, and participate in discussions with experts worldwide.

For instance:

Virtual reality (VR) can take students on a virtual field trip to space, the deep ocean, or historical landmarks.

Online simulations can help students conduct scientific experiments that may not be possible in a traditional classroom.

Gamified learning using educational apps can turn difficult subjects into engaging challenges.

The key is to use technology to enhance learning, not replace traditional methods of thinking and exploration.

A Global Perspective: How Schools Are Innovating Learning

Country	Educational Approach	Key Features
Finland	Student-Centered Learning	No standardized tests, flexible learning, focus on real-world skills
Japan	Collaborative Learning	Peer learning, problem-solving, moral education
Singapore	Inquiry-Based Learning	Focus on questioning, real-world applications

These examples show that schools are evolving—shifting from memorization-based education to experience-based learning.

Bringing Change to Our Own Schools

Education must evolve to keep up with the needs of a rapidly changing world. If schools start incorporating interactive teaching methods, technology, and real-world applications, students will develop the skills needed to think critically, adapt, and innovate.

The question we should ask ourselves is: Are we preparing students for exams, or are we preparing them for life?

The Role of Creativity and Critical Thinking in Learning

In most traditional schools, students are taught what to think rather than how to think. The ability to think critically and creatively is often overlooked, despite being one of the most important skills for success in the real world.

A school that focuses only on exams and memorization does not prepare students for problem-solving, innovation, and adaptability—skills that are essential for personal and professional growth. Creativity and critical thinking should be at the core of education, not an afterthought.

Why Do We Need Critical Thinking in Schools?

Critical thinking is the ability to analyze, question, and evaluate information rather than accepting it at face value. It enables students to make informed decisions, solve complex problems, and develop their own perspectives rather than relying on memorized facts.

For example, in a geography lesson about climate change, students should not just memorize its definition. They should be encouraged to ask deeper questions: What are the real causes of climate change? How does it impact my local community? What solutions can we apply in our own schools or homes? When students engage in such discussions, learning becomes meaningful and connected to real life.

Encouraging Creativity in the Classroom

Creativity is not just for artists and musicians—it is an essential skill for everyone. Creative thinkers are more likely to come up with innovative ideas, adapt to change, and express themselves confidently in different fields.

Some of the world's greatest minds—Albert Einstein, Leonardo da Vinci, and Steve Jobs—were creative thinkers who changed history. They questioned norms, experimented with ideas, and thought differently from others. Schools can foster creativity by encouraging open-ended questions, using brainstorming sessions, and allowing students to experiment and explore rather than just follow rigid guidelines.

A Short Story: The Student Who Solved a Village's Water Crisis

A 14-year-old student, Aarav, lived in a small village where water was scarce. Instead of accepting this as a problem with no solution, he started observing how water was wasted in his community. He realized that rainwater was not being collected effectively.

Using basic materials, Aarav designed a simple but effective rainwater harvesting system for his village school. His idea not only provided a solution to the water crisis but also inspired other students to think about real-world applications of what they learn in school.

This is the power of critical thinking and creativity in education—students stop seeing problems as barriers and start finding solutions.

How Can Schools Integrate Critical Thinking and Creativity?

Many schools around the world are already adopting strategies to nurture these skills. Some methods include:

Project-Based Learning: Instead of passively absorbing information, students work on real-life projects, conduct research, and present their own findings. This method helps students develop hands-on experience and encourages them to think beyond textbooks.

Debates and Discussions: Encouraging students to defend their ideas and engage in discussions sharpens their reasoning and communication skills. A history class, for example, can become more engaging when students debate historical events from different perspectives.

Creative Problem-Solving Activities: Schools can introduce design thinking workshops where students solve real-world problems creatively. For example, students could be asked to create an energy-efficient model home using sustainable materials.

Flexible Learning Methods: Allowing students to explore different ways of expressing their knowledge, such as through art, storytelling, or technology-based projects, helps cater to different learning styles and enhances engagement.

The Importance of Hands-On Learning and Real-World Applications

For decades, schools have relied on textbook-based learning, where students absorb information and reproduce it in exams. However, this approach often fails to connect knowledge with real-life applications. Learning should not be limited to what is written in books; it should be something students can see, experience, and apply in their daily lives.

Imagine learning about gravity only through equations, without ever observing a falling apple, or studying economics without understanding how businesses function in the real world. This disconnect between theory and practice is one of the biggest challenges in modern education.

Why Hands-On Learning is More Effective

When students engage in hands-on activities, they retain knowledge longer and develop problem-solving skills. Studies show that people remember:

- 10% of what they read,
- 20% of what they hear,
- 30% of what they see,
- 50% of what they discuss,
- 75% of what they do, and
- 90% of what they teach others.

This means that learning by doing is far more effective than passively reading or listening to lectures.

A Short Story: The Math Class That Transformed a Village

In a small school in rural India, students struggled with math. They found numbers confusing and formulas difficult to remember. A new teacher, Mrs. Sharma, decided to change the way math was taught. Instead of using a blackboard, she took students to the local market.

She asked them to:

- Calculate the cost of fruits and vegetables.
- Compare prices between different sellers.
- Measure weights using a traditional balance scale.

Suddenly, math became real and practical. Students understood percentages, weight conversions, and profit margins—not because they memorized formulas but because they experienced numbers in action.

Subjects That Benefit Most from Hands-On Learning

While all subjects can integrate real-world applications, certain fields benefit significantly from hands-on methods:

Science and Technology: Laboratory experiments, robotics, and environmental projects help students see science in action.

Mathematics: Applying math in real-world settings—such as budgeting, construction, and data analysis—makes abstract concepts concrete.

History and Social Studies: Field trips to historical sites and interactive storytelling make history come alive.

Entrepreneurship and Business Studies: Simulating businesses, handling real money, and working on market research prepare students for real-world economics.

Environmental Studies: Visiting nature reserves, analyzing waste management, and participating in conservation projects make learning impactful.

A Look at Experiential Learning in Different Countries

Country	Hands-On Learning Approach	Key Features
Germany	Dual Education System	Combines classroom learning with real-world apprenticeships.
United States	Project-Based Learning	Schools emphasize problem-solving through group projects and innovation challenges.
Sweden	Outdoor Education	Students learn science and geography by exploring nature instead of staying in classrooms.

These approaches encourage curiosity, independence, and practical thinking, helping students prepare for life beyond school.

How Schools Can Integrate Real-World Learning

To make learning more engaging and meaningful, schools can adopt methods such as:

Field Visits and Outdoor Learning: Schools can organize visits to factories, farms, courts, media houses, and science museums to give students a direct experience of how industries function.

Community-Based Learning: Encouraging students to identify local problems—such as water shortages or pollution—and come up with innovative solutions builds problem-solving abilities.

Collaborations with Businesses and Experts: Partnering with companies and inviting professionals to share real-world experiences can help students understand how knowledge applies to careers.

Encouraging Student Innovation: Schools can set up makerspaces and innovation labs, where students can create projects, prototypes, and inventions using science and technology.

If we want students to be critical thinkers, innovators, and leaders, we must shift education from memorization to real-world problem-solving. Schools should not just prepare students to pass exams—they should prepare them for life itself.

The State of Government Schools in India: Challenges and Opportunities

Education is a fundamental right, yet millions of children in India face challenges in accessing quality schooling. Government schools, which serve a significant portion of the country's student population, hold immense potential but also encounter hurdles that need thoughtful solutions. With India's growing emphasis on education reforms, this is the perfect moment to explore how we can strengthen our public schooling system and create impactful learning environments.

Understanding the Challenges in Government Schools

One of the biggest challenges in government schools, particularly in rural and remote areas, is the lack of proper infrastructure. Many schools still operate in temporary buildings, with classrooms that lack electricity, ventilation, or basic furniture. A study by the Annual Status of Education Report (ASER) found that nearly 30% of government schools in India do not have functional toilets, and 50% lack access to clean drinking water. These challenges create an environment where students struggle to focus on learning.

Teacher availability and quality are equally crucial. While India has a vast network of teachers, many government schools face faculty shortages. In some remote villages, one teacher handles multiple grades, making personalized attention difficult. Teacher training also plays a vital role. Many educators in rural areas have limited access to modern teaching techniques, which makes it challenging to engage students effectively.

Another significant issue is the accessibility of schools in remote locations. In regions such as Ladakh, Jharkhand, and the Northeastern states, children walk several kilometers daily to reach school. This leads to high dropout rates, particularly among girls. Transport solutions, such as community-based school buses or cycle distribution programs, could significantly improve attendance rates.

Transforming Government Schools: A Path Forward

Despite these challenges, many initiatives have proven that change is possible. With the right investments, partnerships, and innovative approaches, government schools can be transformed into thriving centers of learning. One such example is the successful model of government schools in Kerala, where high literacy rates have been achieved through strong teacher training programs, community involvement, and well-maintained school infrastructure.

Improving infrastructure is a fundamental step. Initiatives like the Atal Tinkering Labs, established under NITI Aayog, have introduced STEM-based learning in government schools, equipping students with hands-on experience in robotics, coding, and science experiments.

Expanding such initiatives to rural schools will bridge the digital divide and provide students with future-ready skills.

Teachers play the most vital role in shaping a student's future. Programs like 'Teach for India' and government-led teacher training workshops have demonstrated that equipping educators with interactive teaching methods improves student engagement. When teachers are provided with continuous learning opportunities, they bring innovation into the classroom.

The Role of Private Schools in Strengthening Education

Private schools are often seen as alternatives to government education, but they can also play a significant role in strengthening the overall learning ecosystem. Many private institutions have successfully implemented innovative learning techniques, modern infrastructure, and digital classrooms. Sharing these best practices with government schools can create a more holistic education system.

Collaborations between private and public schools have already started showing positive results. For example, certain private schools in Delhi and Maharashtra have partnered with nearby government schools to provide mentorship programs, digital learning resources, and joint extracurricular activities. These partnerships foster knowledge exchange and help government schools adopt new-age teaching methods.

A Vision for the Future: Schools That Reach Every Child

Every child deserves quality education, regardless of location or economic background. Transforming government schools is not just a government responsibility—it is a collective effort involving teachers, private institutions, policymakers, and the community. By investing in infrastructure, modernizing teaching methods, and ensuring accessibility, we can create an education system that truly empowers students to shape their future.

As Mahatma Gandhi once said: 'The best way to find yourself is to lose yourself in the service of others.' If we dedicate ourselves to building stronger schools, we will not only uplift students but also contribute to a more knowledgeable and capable society.

CHAPTER 3

College Education – From Degrees to Skills

A college degree has long been considered the key to success in India. For generations, families have placed immense importance on higher education, believing that a degree guarantees respect, financial stability, and career security. But in today's world, is a degree alone enough? With rapid technological advancements and shifting job market demands, the traditional education model is facing serious challenges. The need of the hour is to rethink how colleges prepare students for the future.

India has one of the largest higher education systems in the world, with over 1,000 universities and 42,000 colleges. However, quantity does not always translate to quality. Despite the increasing number of graduates each year, only 48% are considered employable by industry standards. Many degree-holders struggle to secure meaningful jobs, not because they lack intelligence or ambition, but because the education they receive does not equip them with the right skills.

The Indian College Education System: Strengths and Weaknesses

India produces the highest number of engineers and MBA graduates in the world, but paradoxically, many of them lack the practical skills needed for the workplace. The focus of most colleges remains on rote memorization, outdated syllabi, and theory-heavy education. This disconnect between what students learn and what industries require is one of the biggest obstacles to employability.

A study by the National Employability Report highlights some startling facts: nearly 80% of Indian engineering graduates are deemed unemployable in the IT sector due to a lack of hands-on technical skills. Similarly, more than 60% of MBA graduates struggle to find quality jobs, as they often lack real-world business exposure. Over 70% of college courses remain outdated, failing to incorporate emerging industry trends such as artificial intelligence, data science, and digital transformation. If the core structure of higher education remains unchanged, students will continue facing challenges in securing meaningful careers.

A Short Story: The Graduate Who Struggled Despite a Degree

Amit, a bright student from a well-known university, completed his engineering degree with distinction. He had excelled in exams, memorized complex formulas, and submitted well-written assignments. However, when he started applying for jobs, he realized that knowing theories was not enough. Employers were looking for hands-on coding experience, problem-solving abilities, and familiarity with real-world software development.

Amit found himself lagging behind classmates who had taken internships, worked on projects, and learned new-age programming languages through online platforms. While his degree was valuable, it did not equip him with the skills he truly needed in the workplace. Eventually, he had to enroll in additional training programs before he could secure a job. Amit's experience is not unique; it reflects the struggles of thousands of Indian graduates every year.

Why Does This Problem Exist?

The core issue does not lie with students but in the rigid structure of Indian higher education. Colleges often emphasize grades over skills, leading to a system where success is measured by exam scores rather than real-world competency. The traditional approach to education prioritizes theoretical knowledge over practical application, leaving students unprepared for professional challenges.

One of the biggest gaps in the current system is the outdated syllabus. Many courses still follow curriculums designed decades ago, with little consideration for evolving job markets. While the world moves towards automation, digital transformation, and interdisciplinary learning, many Indian colleges continue teaching subjects in isolation without linking them to real-world applications. Without regular updates, students graduate with knowledge that is no longer relevant to modern industries.

Another challenge is the lack of hands-on experience. In most colleges, internships and apprenticeships are either optional or poorly structured. Students rarely get opportunities to apply what they learn in practical settings. In contrast, countries like Germany have successfully implemented dual education systems where students spend half their time in industries, gaining real-world exposure alongside academic learning. If India adopts a similar approach, students would graduate with both knowledge and experience, making them job-ready from day one.

How Can We Improve Indian College Education?

To bridge the gap between education and employability, Indian colleges need to undergo significant transformation. One of the most crucial steps is aligning curriculums with industry demands. Universities must collaborate with leading companies to design courses that reflect current market needs. This includes incorporating subjects like artificial intelligence, business analytics, and sustainable development into mainstream education.

Internships and apprenticeships should become a mandatory part of every degree program. Experience is the strongest factor in employability, and students should not have to wait until graduation to enter the professional world. Colleges must establish partnerships with businesses, startups, and government organizations to provide structured industry training programs. This will help students develop practical skills and professional networks while they are still in college.

Skill-based learning must also take precedence over rote memorization. Degrees are valuable, but they should be complemented by hands-on training in problem-solving, communication, teamwork, and creativity. Colleges should offer certification courses in high-demand fields, ensuring that students graduate with both academic credentials and specialized expertise.

A Look at Global Best Practices

Several countries have successfully moved beyond traditional degrees and embraced skill-based education. Germany's dual education system combines academic coursework with mandatory apprenticeships, allowing students to gain hands-on experience. The United States follows a co-op education model, where universities require students to alternate between academic studies and full-time employment. Finland emphasizes research-based higher education, encouraging students to engage in problem-solving rather than just memorization.

India has already taken steps toward change, with institutions like IITs and IIMs integrating industry partnerships and research-based learning into their programs. However, these reforms need to be expanded across all universities to create a more skilled and adaptable workforce.

The Need for a Practical Approach in Indian Colleges

India's higher education system has expanded significantly, but a critical gap remains between academic learning and practical application. While universities focus heavily on theoretical knowledge, graduates often lack the real-world skills needed for employment. In today's dynamic job market, recruiters prioritize adaptability, problem-solving, and hands-on experience over mere academic scores.

Imagine a mechanical engineering graduate who has studied thermodynamics, machine design, and fluid mechanics extensively but has never assembled or analyzed a real machine. Similarly, a business graduate who excels in financial theory but has never handled market analysis struggles when facing real financial challenges. The inability to apply knowledge practically is one of the biggest hurdles in employability today.

Despite India's impressive college enrollment numbers, many graduates find themselves struggling in the job market. A study by the National Sample Survey Office (NSSO) reveals that over 30% of degree holders remain unemployed, not because of a lack of job openings, but because their education has not equipped them with relevant industry skills.

For instance, an engineering student may score high in exams but struggle to write even basic software code due to a lack of hands-on training. Similarly, an MBA graduate might have an extensive understanding of business theory but fail in professional communication.

A Short Story: The College That Transformed Its Students' Careers

A college in Bengaluru noticed that despite having a well-structured curriculum, its graduates were struggling to secure high-paying jobs. The faculty realized that students were strong in theory but lacked hands-on industry experience. To tackle this, the institution introduced a structured internship program, where final-year students had to work with companies for six months as part of their coursework.

The impact was immediate. Students gained exposure to real projects, interacted with professionals, and learned problem-solving in a workplace setting. By the time they graduated, they had both a degree and relevant industry experience, making them highly sought after by recruiters. This initiative boosted the college's placement rate by 40% in just two years.

How Can We Make Indian Colleges More Industry-Oriented?

Bridging the skill gap in India's college education requires collaborative efforts between academic institutions, industries, and policymakers. The focus must shift from textbook-based learning to a holistic, skill-driven education system.

One crucial aspect is stronger industry-academia collaboration. Colleges should work directly with companies to ensure that students receive real-world exposure. Setting up innovation labs within campuses where students can work on actual industry projects can bridge the gap between academics and practice. Organizing regular guest lectures from industry leaders, facilitating live projects, and mandating industrial training programs will give students a head start before entering the job market.

Another area that needs reform is the examination system. The current method of assessing students through written tests fails to measure their problem-solving abilities. A better approach would be to assess students based on project work, case studies, and real-world applications of their knowledge. Instead of traditional exams, colleges should encourage students to submit working models, business plans, or research papers as part of their final assessments.

Additionally, India needs to expand vocational and technical training. Countries like Germany and Switzerland have successfully implemented dual education models where students split their time between classrooms and industry apprenticeships. By incorporating similar frameworks in Indian colleges, students will graduate with practical experience, reducing unemployment rates and ensuring a more skilled workforce.

Transforming Indian higher education is not a one-step process; it requires continuous evolution. But by introducing industry-relevant courses, modern assessment methods, and real-world training, we can ensure that college degrees once again become a true stepping stone to success.

The Role of Entrepreneurship and Skill-Based Careers in Higher Education

For years, Indian college graduates have followed a conventional path—earning a degree, securing a job, and working for established companies. But today, the world is changing. Entrepreneurship, freelancing, and skill-based careers are gaining momentum, providing alternative paths to success beyond traditional employment.

While India produces over 1.5 million engineers and 3 lakh MBA graduates annually, not all of them find corporate jobs. Instead of waiting for opportunities, many students are now creating their own careers through startups, freelancing, and self-employment. However, most colleges do not prepare students for entrepreneurial thinking, which limits their ability to innovate and take risks.

A Story: The College Dropout Who Built a Multi-Million Business

Rahul, a final-year engineering student, realized that he was more interested in solving real problems than attending lectures. Passionate about technology, he developed an

AI-driven chatbot that could automate customer service for small businesses. Instead of waiting for graduation, he pitched his idea to investors, built a startup, and grew his company while his classmates were still preparing for job interviews.

Within three years, Rahul's startup was valued at ₹50 crores, employing over 100 professionals. His story is not unique—India is home to over 90,000 startups, many founded by young graduates who dared to think differently.

Why Colleges Should Promote Entrepreneurial Thinking

Despite the rising success of startups, most Indian colleges do not teach entrepreneurship as a core subject. Students graduate with theoretical knowledge but lack the practical skills needed to start and run a business. Colleges should:

– Introduce startup incubation centers to help students develop business ideas.
– Offer courses on financial management, leadership, and marketing for future entrepreneurs.
– Connect students with successful entrepreneurs and industry mentors to provide guidance.

By encouraging students to think beyond traditional jobs, colleges can empower them to become job creators rather than job seekers.

Skill-Based Careers: An Alternative to Traditional Degrees

Not every student needs to follow a degree-to-job pipeline. Many high-paying careers today do not require a formal college degree but rather specialized skills and certifications.

For example, digital marketing experts earn salaries comparable to MBA graduates without a business degree. App developers and AI programmers with self-taught coding skills work for global tech giants. Graphic designers and content creators build successful careers through freelancing platforms.

A report by Upwork states that freelancers contribute over $1.2 trillion to the global economy, and India is the second-largest freelance workforce in the world. Yet, very few colleges train students in freelancing or remote work.

Bridging the Gap: What Colleges Can Do

To make students future-ready, colleges should:

- Include freelancing and remote work modules in their curriculum.
- Partner with online education platforms to offer skill-based certifications.
- Encourage students to work on real-world projects to gain experience beyond textbooks.

By reshaping higher education, we can ensure that graduates are equipped not just with degrees but with skills, adaptability, and the confidence to succeed in any career path.

Lessons from Ancient and Medieval Higher Education

Higher education is not a new concept. Long before modern universities existed, ancient civilizations had established centers of learning that focused on holistic development rather than just career preparation. India, in particular, was home to some of the world's earliest and most prestigious institutions, such as Takshashila and Nalanda, which attracted scholars from across the world.

Takshashila, dating back to the 5th century BCE, was not just a university but a hub of intellectual discourse. Unlike modern colleges, admission was based on a student's curiosity and willingness to learn rather than entrance exams. The curriculum covered a wide range of subjects, including medicine, political science, astronomy, and philosophy. Scholars such as Chanakya and Panini, the great Sanskrit grammarian, were associated with this institution.

Similarly, Nalanda University, founded in the 5th century CE, was a global center of knowledge. With over 10,000 students and 2,000 teachers, it had an extensive library containing thousands of manuscripts. Unlike many modern universities where students simply memorize content, Nalanda promoted deep discussions, debates, and logical reasoning. Foreign scholars from China, Korea, and Persia traveled to study in India, highlighting the university's global reputation.

What Can We Learn from Ancient Education?

While technology and job markets have changed, the core principles of true learning remain the same. Modern higher education can learn valuable lessons from ancient institutions:

Holistic Education: Ancient universities focused not just on professional skills but also on philosophy, ethics, and self-development. Modern education should integrate moral and emotional intelligence training.

Discussion-Based Learning: Instead of memorization, ancient education encouraged deep questioning and logical debate. Colleges today should foster a culture where students engage in meaningful discussions rather than just listen to lectures.

Interdisciplinary Approach: Students at Nalanda were encouraged to study multiple disciplines. A similar approach today would prepare students for careers that require adaptability and cross-functional knowledge.

The Psychology of Today's College System

In contrast to ancient education, where students pursued knowledge for its own sake, today's college system is often driven by societal expectations and economic pressures.

Many students see college as a means to an end—a degree that guarantees a job rather than an opportunity for intellectual growth.

When students enter college today, they often experience a mix of emotions—excitement, anxiety, and uncertainty. A survey conducted by the All India Council for Technical Education (AICTE) found that nearly 60% of students enroll in higher education due to parental pressure rather than personal interest. This leads to a lack of motivation and disengagement in learning.

Another challenge is the overwhelming emphasis on grades and placements. Instead of focusing on acquiring real knowledge, students are conditioned to chase high marks, often resorting to rote memorization just to clear exams. This psychological pressure limits creativity and curiosity—two essential qualities that great thinkers and innovators possess.

Bridging the Gap Between Ancient Wisdom and Modern Needs

While modern education cannot function exactly like ancient universities, we can still take inspiration from the past and integrate it into today's system. Universities should promote curiosity-driven learning, encourage students to explore multiple disciplines, and shift the focus from mere certification to holistic personal and intellectual development.

By blending the best aspects of ancient wisdom with the technological advancements of today, we can build a higher education system that not only prepares students for jobs but also for a lifelong journey of knowledge and self-improvement.

The Future of College Education: A New Path Forward

As we stand at the crossroads of rapid technological advancement and shifting job markets, the traditional model of college education must evolve. Degrees alone are no longer enough to secure a successful career—students need adaptable skills, hands-on experience, and the ability to think critically. The future of college education should be a blend of knowledge, innovation, and real-world application.

Reforms Needed for a Stronger College System

To make higher education truly effective, several reforms are needed. The first and most critical change is updating the curriculum to match modern industry demands. Universities should collaborate with industries and professionals to ensure students are learning skills relevant to the job market, rather than outdated theories.

Another significant reform is the **integration of experiential learning** into degree programs. Students should be required to complete internships, industry projects, or research assignments as part of their graduation requirements. This will not only improve employability but also help students transition smoothly from academics to professional life.

Furthermore, education should become **more personalized and flexible**. Online courses, hybrid learning models, and self-paced programs should be made available to accommodate different learning styles. Universities must embrace digital transformation to provide **a dynamic, interactive, and skill-based education experience.**

A Vision for the Future: Beyond Degrees, Towards Lifelong Learning

The future of education is not just about earning a degree—it's about becoming a lifelong learner. Successful professionals of tomorrow will not just rely on what they learned in college but will continue upskilling throughout their careers. Institutions should encourage students to develop a mindset of continuous learning, adaptability, and problem-solving.

A well-rounded higher education system should balance **technical knowledge, critical thinking, creativity, and ethical awareness.** Rather than focusing solely on exam scores, universities should nurture students into independent thinkers who can contribute meaningfully to society.

As the great philosopher Socrates once said, 'Education is the kindling of a flame, not the filling of a vessel.' The goal of college education should not just be to impart information but to ignite a passion for learning, discovery, and innovation.

CHAPTER 4

Emotional Intelligence and Its Importance for Teenagers

As a teacher, I have had countless conversations with my students — some about academics, some about their dreams, and some about the silent battles they fight within themselves. What has always stood out to me is how many of them struggle to understand and express their emotions. I have seen students break down in frustration because they couldn't name what they were feeling. I have witnessed bright, talented children withdraw into silence, not because they lacked the ability to speak, but because they felt no one would truly listen.

What pains me the most is that many of these students carry their emotional burdens alone. Whether it's fear of being misunderstood, the belief that showing emotions is a sign of weakness, or simply the absence of a safe space where they can open up — these barriers keep them from seeking help. And so, their emotions remain bottled up, hidden behind forced smiles and restless silences.

These experiences have shaped my understanding of emotional intelligence, not as a mere skill to be taught, but as a critical life lesson that every learner deserves to embrace. I believe that before we expect our students to excel academically, we must first help them become emotionally aware, resilient, and expressive.

"Emotional intelligence is not the opposite of intelligence, it is not the triumph of heart over head – it is the unique intersection of both."

– David Caruso

In today's fast-paced world, intelligence is often measured by academic achievements and technical skills. However, research has shown that emotional intelligence (EQ) is just as important—if not more—than IQ when it comes to personal and professional success. Emotional intelligence is the ability to understand, manage, and express emotions in a healthy way. It also involves recognizing and understanding the emotions of others, which helps build strong relationships and effective communication skills.

Teenagers, in particular, go through significant emotional and psychological changes. From academic pressures to social challenges, their ability to navigate emotions plays a crucial role in their well-being. Developing emotional intelligence helps students handle stress, make better decisions, and interact with others more effectively.

The Key Components of Emotional Intelligence

Psychologist Daniel Goleman, who popularized the concept of emotional intelligence, identified five main components that shape a person's EQ:

1. Self-Awareness

Self-awareness is the ability to recognize and understand one's emotions. When students are aware of their emotions, they can identify triggers that cause stress, frustration, or happiness. This awareness allows them to respond to situations more thoughtfully instead of reacting impulsively.

2. Self-Regulation

Managing emotions is just as important as recognizing them. Self-regulation helps students control their impulses, stay calm under pressure, and adapt to changing situations. For example, instead of getting angry when faced with a difficult exam, a student with strong self-regulation skills will take a deep breath, focus, and approach the challenge with a clear mind.

3. Motivation

Motivation goes beyond external rewards like grades or recognition. It involves an internal drive to achieve goals, improve oneself, and stay resilient in the face of obstacles. Students with high emotional intelligence are often self-motivated, which helps them maintain a positive attitude toward learning and growth.

4. Empathy

Empathy is the ability to understand and share the feelings of others. It helps students build meaningful relationships, resolve conflicts peacefully, and support their peers. A student who is empathetic can sense when a friend is struggling and offer comfort or assistance.

5. Social Skills

Strong social skills enable students to communicate effectively, collaborate with others, and build lasting friendships. Whether it's working in a team, expressing opinions respectfully, or resolving disagreements, social skills are essential for both personal and professional success.

Emotional Intelligence vs. IQ: Which Matters More?

For a long time, intelligence was primarily associated with IQ, which measures logical reasoning, memory, and problem-solving abilities. However, studies have found that IQ alone does not determine success. Many people with high IQs struggle with interpersonal relationships, decision-making, and emotional control. In contrast, individuals with strong emotional intelligence are more likely to lead successful and fulfilling lives.

A student with a high IQ may excel in academics, but without emotional intelligence, they may struggle to manage stress, work in teams, or handle criticism. On the other hand, a student with strong EQ can navigate challenges, communicate effectively, and maintain strong personal and professional relationships.

Developing emotional intelligence is not just about becoming a better student—it's about becoming a better person. In the following sections, we will explore how students can improve their emotional intelligence and apply it to everyday life.

Emotional Intelligence and Managing Stress

Stress is a common part of student life, whether it's due to academic pressure, peer expectations, or personal challenges. However, how students handle stress makes a significant difference in their overall well-being. Emotional intelligence plays a key role in managing stress by helping students recognize their emotions, control their reactions, and develop healthy coping strategies.

Students with strong emotional intelligence can identify the signs of stress early and take proactive steps to manage it. Instead of feeling overwhelmed by exams or deadlines, they break tasks into smaller, manageable goals. Rather than reacting negatively to setbacks, they analyze the situation, learn from it, and move forward with a positive mindset.

The Connection Between Emotional Intelligence and Mental Well-Being

Emotional intelligence is directly linked to mental health. Students who understand their emotions and express them in a healthy way are less likely to suffer from anxiety, depression, or self-doubt. When they experience negative emotions, they do not suppress them; instead, they process them constructively, seeking support from friends, family, or teachers when needed.

Additionally, emotional intelligence helps students develop resilience—the ability to bounce back from difficulties. Whether it's a poor exam score, a disagreement with a friend, or a personal failure, students with high EQ view challenges as opportunities to grow rather than as reasons to give up. They understand that setbacks are a part of life and that emotional strength comes from learning how to handle them.

The Role of Emotional Intelligence in Friendships and Social Interactions

Friendships are an essential part of student life, and emotional intelligence plays a major role in building and maintaining healthy relationships. A person with high emotional intelligence understands not only their own emotions but also those of others. This helps them communicate effectively, resolve misunderstandings, and show empathy toward their peers.

Students with strong EQ are more likely to form deep and meaningful friendships because they can listen actively, support others, and handle social situations with maturity. They also tend to attract positive relationships, as people naturally gravitate toward those who are kind, understanding, and emotionally stable.

Building Confidence and Self-Esteem Through Emotional Intelligence

Confidence and self-esteem are closely linked to emotional intelligence. When students understand and manage their emotions, they feel more in control of their actions and decisions. They are less likely to be affected by negative criticism and more likely to believe in their own abilities.

For example, a student with strong EQ will not let a single bad grade define their self-worth. Instead of feeling discouraged, they will analyze what went wrong, learn from their mistakes, and work toward improvement. Similarly, in social situations, emotionally intelligent students do not let others' opinions shake their confidence. They know who they are and remain true to their values.

Developing self-confidence also involves positive self-talk. Instead of saying, 'I can't do this,' a student with high EQ would say, 'I am still learning, and I will get better.' These small shifts in mindset make a huge difference in how students view themselves and their capabilities.

Handling Conflicts and Disagreements Using Emotional Intelligence

Conflicts are a natural part of life, but how we handle them determines the outcome. Many students struggle with disagreements, whether it's with friends, teachers, or family members. Emotional intelligence helps in resolving conflicts peacefully by promoting understanding, patience, and effective communication.

One key aspect of conflict resolution is active listening. Instead of reacting defensively, an emotionally intelligent person listens carefully to the other person's point of view before responding. This helps in finding common ground and avoiding unnecessary arguments.

Another important skill is managing emotions during a disagreement. Instead of letting anger take over, students with high EQ take a step back, assess the situation, and respond rationally. They focus on solving the problem rather than proving themselves right. This leads to healthier relationships and mutual respect.

By applying emotional intelligence in social interactions, students can build stronger friendships, develop confidence, and resolve conflicts in a mature and respectful way. These skills not only make student life smoother but also prepare them for success in their future careers and relationships.

The Role of Parents and Teachers in Developing Emotional Intelligence

Emotional intelligence is not something students develop on their own; it is nurtured by the people around them. Parents and teachers play a crucial role in helping young minds understand and manage emotions. **When adults demonstrate emotional awareness, patience, and kindness, students naturally learn to do the same.**

Parents can support their children's emotional growth by encouraging open conversations. Instead of dismissing a child's emotions, they should listen actively, acknowledge their feelings, and help them process emotions in a healthy way. Simple practices like asking, 'How was your day?' or discussing challenges in a non-judgmental manner create a safe space for emotional expression.

Teachers, on the other hand, can create classroom environments that promote emotional intelligence. Instead of just focusing on academics, they can incorporate social-emotional learning into lessons. Encouraging teamwork, resolving conflicts peacefully, and discussing emotions in a structured way all help students develop self-awareness and empathy. Teachers who practice patience and understanding set an example for students to follow.

"We teach students to solve equations, but forget to teach them to solve the storms inside their hearts."

Let me share a brief fictional narrative

Aarav was a 15-year-old boy, studying in Class 10. From the outside, his life looked normal. He went to school every day, played cricket with his friends, and scrolled through his phone like every other teenager. But inside his heart, there was a lot happening — something nobody could see.

Sometimes Aarav felt very angry, even for small reasons. Sometimes he felt sad without understanding why. There were days he wanted to cry, but tears just didn't come out. At home, his parents were always busy with work. They asked him about homework, marks, and tests, but never about how he felt. Aarav wanted to talk, but every time he thought of sharing his feelings, a voice in his mind stopped him — "What if they don't understand?" "What if they think I am weak?"

Slowly, Aarav started keeping everything inside his heart. He laughed with his friends, but the smile was fake. He was carrying a heavy weight of emotions, but no one knew.

One day, after a small argument, Aarav shouted at his best friend Rohit. The argument was about a cricket match, but Aarav's anger came from somewhere deeper. Later that night, when he lay on his bed, Aarav felt guilty and confused. "Why did I shout so much?" "Why do I feel so restless all the time?" He had no answers.

The next day, something special happened. Aarav's class teacher, Mrs. Meera, gave a simple task. "Today, I want each of you to write a letter to yourself. Write whatever you feel. No one will read it — only you." Aarav felt strange. What was the point? But as he started writing, something changed. Slowly, all the feelings he had locked inside began to come out.

He wrote about his fears — fear of failing, fear of disappointing his parents, fear of being alone. He wrote about his anger, his sadness, his confusion. By the end of the letter, Aarav felt lighter, as if he had put down a huge burden.

The next day, Mrs. Meera spoke about emotional intelligence. She explained that it means understanding our own feelings, accepting them, and learning how to manage them. It also means understanding the feelings of others. Aarav listened carefully. For the first time, someone was teaching him about emotions — something he really needed.

Slowly, Aarav started practicing small things. When he felt angry, he asked himself "Why am I angry? What is really bothering me?" When he felt sad, he allowed himself to feel it instead of hiding it. When his friends looked upset, he didn't make fun of them. He asked, "Are you okay?"

Aarav still had bad days sometimes, but now, he understood his feelings better. He didn't feel lost all the time. He learned that it is okay to feel every emotion — even sadness, anger, or fear — because feelings are not enemies. They are messages. They tell us something is important to us.

Aarav's story is simple, but it is important. Many teenagers feel the same storm inside, but they don't know how to deal with it. Emotional intelligence gave Aarav the courage to understand himself and to help others too. And that's the first step to becoming a strong and happy person.

Creating Classroom Environments That Support Emotional Growth

A school should not just be a place for intellectual learning; it should also foster emotional growth. Classrooms that encourage collaboration, open discussions, and respect for different perspectives create emotionally intelligent students. Schools can introduce group activities where students work together to solve problems, engage in storytelling exercises that highlight empathy, or practice mindfulness techniques to manage stress.

Additionally, schools should recognize the importance of emotional well-being. Counseling services, student support groups, and mental health awareness programs can make a huge difference in a student's ability to handle emotions. When students feel emotionally safe and supported, they perform better academically and socially.

Exercises and Activities to Improve Emotional Intelligence

Like any skill, emotional intelligence improves with practice. Students can develop their EQ through simple yet effective activities. Here are a few exercises that can help:

1. Emotion Journaling: Writing down daily emotions helps students recognize patterns in their feelings and understand what triggers certain emotions. This builds self-awareness.
2. Role-Playing Scenarios: Practicing different social situations, such as resolving conflicts or expressing gratitude, helps students improve their communication and empathy skills.
3. Mindfulness and Deep Breathing: Learning how to manage emotions through breathing exercises and mindfulness practices can reduce stress and improve focus.

4. Acts of Kindness: Encouraging students to perform small acts of kindness, like helping a classmate or writing a thank-you note, strengthens their ability to connect with others.

By integrating these exercises into daily routines, students can develop strong emotional intelligence skills that will help them in school, relationships, and future careers. Emotional intelligence is not just an academic skill—it is a life skill that shapes a person's happiness, success, and ability to create positive relationships.

Emotional Intelligence: A Key to Success and Happiness

In today's world, emotional intelligence is no longer just an advantage—it is a necessity. While academic achievements and technical skills are important, the ability to manage emotions, communicate effectively, and build meaningful relationships plays an equally vital role in personal and professional success. Emotional intelligence helps individuals navigate challenges with confidence, adapt to changes, and build a fulfilling life.

Research has shown that people with high EQ tend to be more successful in leadership roles, workplace environments, and personal relationships. They have better decision-making skills, stronger resilience, and an ability to work well under pressure. Unlike IQ, which remains relatively stable throughout life, emotional intelligence can be developed and improved with time and practice.

The Influence of EQ on Leadership and Decision-Making

One of the most significant benefits of emotional intelligence is its impact on leadership. Great leaders are not just intelligent—they are emotionally aware, empathetic, and capable of inspiring others. They understand the emotions of the people around them, making them effective communicators and decision-makers.

For students, developing leadership skills through emotional intelligence means learning to listen, collaborate, and take responsibility. Whether leading a group project, supporting a friend, or taking initiative in a classroom, emotional intelligence allows students to handle responsibilities with maturity and wisdom.

A Lifelong Journey of Growth and Learning

Emotional intelligence is not just a skill for school—it is a lifelong tool that continues to shape personal growth. As students transition into adulthood, their ability to manage emotions, build strong relationships, and make thoughtful decisions will define their path to success. The habits they develop now—such as self-awareness, empathy, and resilience—will guide them through every stage of life.

A person with strong emotional intelligence is not just intelligent on paper; they are kind, understanding, and respected by others. They know how to handle stress, resolve conflicts peacefully, and find balance in their personal and professional lives. This is why emotional intelligence should not be an afterthought—it should be at the core of education and personal development.

A Final Message: Prioritizing Emotional Intelligence

To students, developing emotional intelligence will empower you to overcome challenges, build confidence, and create meaningful connections with others. It will help you not only succeed academically but also live a fulfilling and balanced life.

To parents, your support and guidance play a crucial role in shaping your child's emotional intelligence. Encourage open discussions, lead by example, and create an environment where emotions are acknowledged and understood.

To educators, emotional intelligence should be an integral part of teaching. By fostering self-awareness, empathy, and communication in students, you are preparing them not just for exams but for life itself.

In the end, intelligence alone does not define success—emotional intelligence does. The ability to understand emotions, connect with people, and handle challenges with wisdom is what truly sets individuals apart. Let us all work toward making emotional intelligence a priority so that future generations can lead with compassion, resilience, and purpose.

CHAPTER 5

The Importance of Ethics for Young Minds

Once, I gave my students a situation to discuss:

"You witness a group of seniors bullying a younger student behind the school building. The younger student is crying, but too scared to speak up. You are not directly involved, but you saw everything. What will you do?"

I didn't ask for answers immediately. I simply let the silence settle in the classroom, allowing the weight of the situation to sink in. Ethics is not about theoretical right and wrong — it's about what we choose to do when faced with uncomfortable truths. Will you stand up, stay silent, or walk away? These are not just school situations; these are life's real tests, and how we respond shapes who we become.

Some weeks after that discussion, a student walked up to me after class. In her hand was a crumpled ₹100 note. She said, "Sir, I found this near the water cooler. What should I do?"

I smiled and asked, "What do you think is the right thing to do?"

Without hesitation, she replied, "It's not mine, so it belongs to someone else. I think we should announce it tomorrow so the owner can take it."

That was a proud moment — not because she found the right answer, but because she trusted her inner voice to guide her. This is what ethics education looks like — not lectures, but small moments where children learn to listen to their conscience and act with integrity.

Education is not just about learning facts and acquiring skills—it is also about shaping character. Moral education plays a crucial role in helping students understand values such as honesty, responsibility, kindness, and fairness. In a world that is becoming increasingly complex, students need ethical guidance to make the right choices, interact positively with others, and become responsible members of society.

In recent years, a disturbing trend has emerged among some young people — finding entertainment in cruelty. Bullying classmates, disrespecting and mocking elders, and even abusing animals have become content for viral videos. Instead of feeling compassion for the victim, many laugh, cheer, and share these moments online, treating humiliation and pain as a form of comedy. This shift reflects a deeper crisis — a loss of empathy and ethical grounding. When disrespect and cruelty become sources of entertainment, we are not just normalizing bad behavior — we are celebrating it. This is why ethical education is no longer optional — it has become a necessary shield to protect young minds from growing numb to kindness, responsibility, and respect.

This is not just mischief — this is a serious ethical drift. When children start enjoying the pain of others, we are not just failing as educators, we are failing as a society. If we do not step in now and rebuild that sense of compassion, fairness, and respect, we are raising a generation that might succeed academically, but fail as human beings.

Ethics is not an 'extra subject' for moral science periods. It is the invisible curriculum that shapes how students think, speak, act, and most importantly — how they treat others. A child who learns to cheat in school will find it easier to cheat at work. A child who learns to mock others' pain will find it easier to bully in adulthood. And a child who learns to stay silent in the face of wrong will grow into an adult who looks the other way when injustice happens.

As educators and parents, our responsibility goes far beyond grades. We are shaping not just careers, but character.

"Education without values, as useful as it is, seems rather to make man a more clever devil."

– C.S. Lewis

The importance of moral education goes beyond individual behavior. A society that fosters strong ethical values in its youth creates a more harmonious and just world. When students learn to differentiate between right and wrong, they become more compassionate, respectful, and conscious of their impact on others. Ethics shape how they treat friends, family, and even strangers, building a foundation of integrity that lasts a lifetime.

How Ethics Shape Character and Decision-Making

A student's moral foundation influences their decision-making process in every aspect of life. Whether it is choosing to stand up against bullying, taking responsibility for mistakes, or being truthful in difficult situations, ethical values guide these choices. When students develop a strong sense of morality, they learn to think critically about their actions and understand the consequences of their behavior.

Ethics also play a significant role in professional and personal success. Employers value honesty, reliability, and teamwork—qualities that are deeply rooted in moral education. A person who acts with integrity earns trust and respect, paving the way for long-term growth in both career and relationships. By instilling strong ethical values in students, we are preparing them not only for academic success but also for the challenges of real life.

Why Schools Should Prioritize Moral Education

Despite its importance, moral education is often overlooked in school curriculums. Many schools focus solely on academic achievements, leaving little room for ethical discussions. However, education should not be limited to knowledge—it should also nurture kindness, compassion, and social responsibility. Schools that integrate moral education create a more positive learning environment, where students respect one another and develop strong interpersonal skills.

Moral education should not be taught as a separate subject but rather integrated into everyday learning. Schools can incorporate ethics into history, literature, and science discussions, helping students analyze moral dilemmas and reflect on their values. Teachers and parents play a vital role in this process, as young minds often learn morality by observing the actions of adults around them.

In the end, academic excellence alone is not enough to build a successful and fulfilling life. True education includes both intellectual and moral development. By teaching students not just how to be smart but also how to be good, we create a generation of responsible citizens who will contribute positively to society.

Moral Education and the Power of Empathy

One of the greatest benefits of moral education is that it fosters empathy—the ability to understand and share the feelings of others. Empathy is the foundation of a compassionate and harmonious society. When students are taught to see the world from different perspectives, they develop a sense of responsibility toward others. This helps reduce bullying, discrimination, and conflicts, creating a more inclusive environment both in schools and in society.

Empathy also enhances communication skills and teamwork. In today's interconnected world, the ability to work with people from different backgrounds is essential. Students who learn to appreciate diversity and respect different opinions become more open-minded and adaptable. By incorporating moral education into daily lessons, we can help students grow into individuals who not only excel academically but also contribute to making the world a better place.

The Role of Teachers and Parents in Teaching Ethics

Moral education cannot be taught through textbooks alone—it is best learned through real-life examples. Teachers and parents play a crucial role in shaping a child's ethical values. Children observe the actions of the adults around them, and they learn from what they see rather than just from what they are told. If a child sees honesty, kindness, and respect practiced at home and in school, they are more likely to adopt these values.

Teachers can integrate ethics into daily lessons by encouraging discussions about moral dilemmas, historical events, and literature that highlight ethical conflicts. Parents, on the other hand, can reinforce these lessons by having open conversations about values and decision-making. For instance, instead of simply telling a child to be honest, parents can share personal experiences where honesty led to positive outcomes. These small yet meaningful interactions have a lasting impact on a child's moral development.

Storytelling: A Powerful Tool for Teaching Morality

Stories have been used for centuries to teach moral lessons. From ancient fables to modern-day literature, storytelling is one of the most effective ways to impart values in young minds. When children hear stories about honesty, courage, and kindness, they relate to the characters and understand the consequences of ethical and unethical behavior.

By combining empathy, real-life examples, and storytelling, moral education can become an integral part of a student's learning journey. These values do not just help students in their academic years but stay with them throughout their lives, shaping them into responsible and ethical individuals.

Moral Education and Ethical Decision-Making in Real Life

Education is not just about acquiring knowledge—it is about learning how to make the right choices. Every day, students face situations where they must decide between what is easy and what is right. Whether it is being honest about a mistake, standing up for someone who is being mistreated, or resisting negative peer pressure, moral education equips students with the ability to make ethical decisions in real life.

A strong moral foundation helps students evaluate situations critically. When they are faced with ethical dilemmas, they do not simply follow the crowd but instead analyze the possible consequences of their actions. Moral education encourages students to ask questions like: 'Is this the right thing to do?' 'Will my actions harm others?' and 'Am I being honest and fair?'. These questions guide them toward making responsible and thoughtful decisions.

The Influence of Peers and Social Media on Morality

In today's world, students are constantly influenced by their peers and social media. While friendships are important, peer pressure can sometimes lead to poor decision-making. Many students find themselves making choices based on what others expect rather than what they truly believe is right. This is why moral education is essential—it gives students the confidence to say no to negative influences and stand by their values.

Social media plays a powerful role in shaping young minds. The constant exposure to different opinions, trends, and influencers can impact how students perceive right and wrong. Unfortunately, social media also spreads misinformation and promotes unhealthy behaviors. Without a strong moral compass, students may struggle to differentiate between what is ethical and what is not. By teaching digital ethics—such as responsible online behavior, respect for others' privacy, and the ability to recognize fake news—moral education helps students navigate the digital world responsibly.

Building a Strong Moral Foundation for Life

Moral education should not be something students forget once they leave school. It should be a lifelong guide that helps them in personal relationships, careers, and society. To build a lasting moral foundation, students must not only learn ethical principles but also practice them daily.

One way to reinforce moral values is through reflection. Encouraging students to think about their actions and their impact on others helps them internalize ethical behavior. Schools and families can create opportunities for students to discuss moral challenges they have faced and explore different ways to handle them.

Acts of kindness, honesty, and respect should be encouraged and celebrated. When students see that ethical behavior is valued, they are more likely to adopt these habits naturally. Schools can integrate service-learning projects, mentorship programs, and leadership activities that reinforce the importance of integrity in daily life.

By equipping students with the tools to make ethical decisions, resist negative influences, and practice moral values in everyday life, we prepare them for a future where they can positively impact the world. The goal of moral education is not just to create good students but to nurture good human beings.

Moral Education and Leadership: Shaping Responsible Citizens

Leadership is not just about authority; it is about responsibility. A true leader is someone who makes ethical decisions, inspires others, and acts with integrity. Moral education plays a crucial role in shaping young leaders by teaching them the value of honesty, fairness, and accountability. When students understand the importance of ethical leadership, they develop the confidence to take initiative, help others, and create positive change.

History has shown us that great leaders are not just those who are knowledgeable, but those who have strong moral values. Figures like Mahatma Gandhi, Nelson Mandela, and Martin Luther King Jr. are remembered not just for their intelligence, but for their ethical principles and unwavering commitment to justice. By incorporating moral education into school curriculums, we can help students develop qualities that prepare them to lead with wisdom and compassion.

The Role of Moral Values in Creating a Better Society

A society is only as strong as the values of its people. When moral education is prioritized, communities become more respectful, tolerant, and just. Students who learn the importance of kindness, responsibility, and fairness grow into adults who contribute positively to society. They become individuals who respect laws, uphold justice, and work toward social harmony.

One of the biggest challenges in today's world is the rise of unethical behavior in various fields—whether in business, politics, or everyday life. Corruption, dishonesty, and selfishness often create problems that affect entire communities. Moral education serves as a strong foundation that prevents these issues by shaping ethical citizens from a young age. A society built on strong moral values is one that thrives in trust, cooperation, and progress.

Preparing Students for Real-World Ethical Challenges

Life presents various ethical dilemmas, and students need to be prepared to handle them. Whether it is making ethical choices at work, maintaining integrity in relationships, or standing up for justice, moral education provides the tools to navigate these challenges wisely.

For example, in professional settings, employees often face ethical decisions such as choosing between profit and fairness, truth and deception, or individual success and team well-being. Those who have a strong moral foundation make decisions that benefit not just themselves, but also the people around them. Ethical behavior builds trust, strengthens relationships, and ultimately leads to long-term success.

By integrating moral education into school systems, we are not just preparing students for exams—we are preparing them for life. A world where individuals act with honesty, kindness, and responsibility is a world that progresses toward peace and prosperity. Education should not only teach students how to earn a living but also how to live with purpose and integrity.

Moral Education: A Foundation for Life

Moral education is not just a subject to be taught in schools—it is a foundation for a meaningful and fulfilling life. It shapes our thoughts, influences our decisions, and defines the kind of individuals we become. In a world where success is often measured by material achievements, moral education reminds us that true success lies in integrity, compassion, and the impact we have on others.

As students grow, the lessons of moral education extend beyond the classroom. In careers, honesty and ethical behavior build trust and reputation. In relationships, values like kindness and respect create meaningful connections. In leadership, a strong moral compass ensures decisions are made with fairness and justice. The values learned in youth guide us through every stage of life, helping us navigate challenges and shape a better world.

The Lifelong Impact of Ethical Learning

Every great society is built upon the values of its people. When moral education is given priority, future generations grow up with a sense of responsibility, fairness, and empathy. This leads to a world where individuals treat each other with respect, leaders make decisions for the greater good, and businesses operate with honesty and fairness.

The true test of a person's character is not how they behave when things are easy, but how they act in difficult situations. Those with strong moral values do not compromise their principles for temporary gain. They choose to do what is right, even when no one is watching. Such individuals not only achieve personal success but also inspire others to follow the path of integrity.

Embracing Moral Education

To students, moral education is your guide to becoming the best version of yourself. It will help you build confidence, make ethical decisions, and earn the trust of those around you. Embrace these values, and you will find that success is not just about what you achieve, but also about how you achieve it.

To parents, remember that children learn more from what they see than from what they hear. Be the role models that guide them toward kindness, honesty, and responsibility. Your actions will leave a lasting impression on their character.

To educators, teaching moral education is just as important as teaching science, mathematics, or literature. By nurturing ethical values in students, you are preparing them to lead with wisdom and compassion. You are shaping the future, one lesson at a time.

In the race to secure the brightest future for our children, we often forget to ensure that they grow into good human beings first. The success of a student should not just be measured in marksheets and medals, but in the strength of their conscience — in the courage to stand for what is right, the compassion to uplift others, and the honesty to choose the harder right over the easier wrong. Moral education is not about preaching rules — it is about planting seeds of empathy, honesty, respect, and courage so that even when no one is watching, they choose to do what is right. When children understand that their actions shape not just their own future, but the world around them, we create a generation that doesn't just succeed — it inspires, heals, and leads with heart.

"A brilliant mind without a kind heart is like a sharp knife in the wrong hands — dangerous, unpredictable, and destructive."

CHAPTER 6

The Role of Teachers – Beyond Just Instructors

Teachers have always been at the heart of education. They do more than just impart knowledge—they inspire, guide, and shape the future of society. From ancient times to modern classrooms, the role of teachers has evolved significantly. In today's rapidly changing world, teachers are no longer just instructors; they are mentors, motivators, and facilitators of learning.

A teacher's influence extends far beyond textbooks and exams. A great teacher can ignite curiosity in students, encourage them to think critically, and give them the confidence to explore new ideas. The impact of a teacher often lasts a lifetime—many successful individuals credit their achievements to the inspiration and support of a great educator.

"A teacher is never ordinary; both destruction and creation rest in their hands."

– Chanakya

The Evolution of Teaching: From Gurukuls to Digital Classrooms

Education has transformed over centuries, and so has the role of teachers. In ancient India, the Gurukul system emphasized personalized mentorship, where students lived with their teachers, learning not just academics but also life skills and values. Knowledge was transferred through discussions, practical application, and deep understanding.

In contrast, modern classrooms are structured around curriculums, grades, and standardized testing. While this system has made education more accessible, it has also created challenges—teachers are often burdened with administrative tasks, large class sizes, and rigid syllabi, leaving little room for personalized learning.

With the rise of technology, education is now moving towards digital and interactive learning environments. Teachers today are expected to integrate online tools, multimedia content, and global resources to make learning engaging and effective. The challenge is to balance technology with the human connection that makes teaching a deeply personal and impactful profession.

What Makes a Great Teacher?

A great teacher is more than just someone who explains concepts; they create an environment where students feel encouraged to learn, question, and explore. Some qualities that define an exceptional teacher include:

Empathy and Patience: Understanding that every student learns differently and providing support accordingly.

Passion for Teaching: Bringing enthusiasm into the classroom and making subjects interesting.

Adaptability: Being open to new teaching methods, technology, and student needs.

Encouraging Critical Thinking: Teaching students how to think rather than what to think.

Mentorship Beyond Academics: Guiding students in their personal and emotional growth, not just in studies.

Beyond Academics: The Teacher's Role in Shaping Lives

A teacher's role extends far beyond the walls of a classroom. While academic instruction remains at the core of teaching, a true educator does much more than just deliver lessons. They become mentors, role models, and even second parents to their students. A teacher's responsibility is not only to educate but also to inspire, encourage, and guide students through the challenges of life. Education is not just about passing exams; it is about preparing young minds for the real world, helping them develop critical thinking, emotional resilience, and moral integrity.

One of the greatest contributions a teacher makes is fostering curiosity and creativity. The best educators do not just dictate facts; they encourage students to ask questions, challenge conventional wisdom, and explore beyond the textbook. By creating an environment where students feel safe to express their thoughts and ideas, teachers help young minds develop the confidence to think independently. A teacher who encourages curiosity does not just create a good student; they create a lifelong learner. This is particularly important in today's world, where knowledge is constantly evolving, and students must be adaptable and open to continuous learning.

Another crucial role teachers play is in emotional and social development. Many children and teenagers struggle with personal challenges—family issues, peer pressure, self-doubt, or anxiety about the future. A compassionate teacher recognizes these challenges and provides the necessary support and guidance. Sometimes, a simple act of kindness from a teacher—a few words of encouragement, an understanding conversation, or a moment of patience—can make a lasting difference in a student's life. A good teacher understands that learning is not just about intellect; it is also about emotional well-being.

Teachers are also instrumental in shaping students' values and ethics. In a world that is rapidly changing, with increasing exposure to social media and external influences, it is crucial for students to develop a strong moral compass. Teachers who instill values like honesty, empathy, respect, and responsibility in their students contribute to building a more ethical and compassionate society. While subjects like science, mathematics, and literature are essential, character development is equally important, and a good teacher recognizes the balance between knowledge and values.

The Challenges Teachers Face and How We Can Support Them

Despite their critical role in shaping the future, teachers often face numerous challenges. One of the most significant challenges is the increasing burden of administrative work. Many teachers today spend a considerable amount of time handling paperwork, grading assignments, and fulfilling institutional requirements, which leaves them with less time to focus on actual teaching and mentoring. This overburdened system often leads to burnout, reducing the effectiveness and enthusiasm of even the most passionate educators.

Another major challenge is the lack of resources and support, particularly in government schools and rural areas. Many teachers work in classrooms with inadequate infrastructure, outdated textbooks, and limited access to digital learning tools. Teaching effectively in such environments requires incredible dedication and creativity. It is essential for governments, educational institutions, and communities to come together to provide teachers with the necessary support, training, and resources they need to create a more engaging and effective learning experience.

Beyond external challenges, teachers also face the difficult task of keeping students engaged in an era of distractions. With the rise of smartphones, social media, and digital entertainment, capturing a student's attention has become more difficult than ever. A modern teacher must learn to integrate technology into their teaching methods rather than fight against it. The use of interactive lessons, educational apps, and real-world examples can make learning more exciting and relevant to students. However, this also means that teachers themselves need continuous learning and adaptation to stay ahead in this rapidly evolving educational landscape.

To support teachers, society must recognize and respect their efforts. Teaching should not be seen merely as a profession but as a pillar of nation-building. Increasing salaries, reducing workload, and offering more professional development opportunities are some ways to uplift the teaching community. More importantly, fostering a culture where teachers are appreciated and valued will encourage more talented individuals to take up teaching as a career, ultimately benefiting the education system as a whole.

Teaching is one of the few professions where a single individual has the power to influence hundreds of lives each year. A great teacher does not just teach a subject; they teach students how to learn, how to think, and how to grow. In a world that constantly needs new ideas, new leaders, and new solutions, teachers remain the guiding force that ensures the next generation is ready to take on the future.

The Teacher-Student Relationship: A Key to Meaningful Learning

Education is not just about textbooks and exams; it is also about the bond between teachers and students. A strong teacher-student relationship can transform a student's learning experience, making education more engaging, enjoyable, and impactful. When students feel understood and respected by their teachers, they become more confident, curious, and eager to learn. This connection can inspire students to push beyond their limits, discover their potential, and develop a lifelong love for learning.

A teacher who is approachable and empathetic creates an environment where students feel safe to ask questions and express their thoughts. This encourages open discussions, leading to deeper understanding and critical thinking. In contrast, when students fear their teachers or feel ignored, they hesitate to participate, leading to passive learning and disinterest in education. Teachers who build strong connections with their students do not just impart knowledge; they help shape personalities, boost self-esteem, and instill a sense of responsibility.

The Influence of Teaching Styles on Student Engagement

Different teachers have different styles of teaching, and each style impacts students in unique ways. A teacher who relies solely on lecturing may find it difficult to keep students engaged, while one who incorporates real-life examples, storytelling, and interactive discussions can make lessons more relatable and memorable. The most effective teachers adapt their teaching styles to meet the needs of their students, using a mix of traditional and modern methods to create a dynamic learning environment.

For instance, some teachers use the 'Socratic method,' where they ask thought-provoking questions instead of simply providing answers. This method encourages students to think critically, analyze problems, and develop their own perspectives. Others prefer a hands-on approach, where students learn by doing rather than just listening. In science classes, for example, experiments and practical demonstrations help students grasp concepts more effectively than theory alone. Teachers who understand the importance of adapting their approach based on their students' needs create classrooms that are both informative and inspiring.

The Role of Emotional Intelligence in Teaching

A great teacher is not only knowledgeable but also emotionally intelligent. Emotional intelligence—the ability to understand and manage emotions—plays a crucial role in teaching. Students come from different backgrounds and experiences, and a teacher who can recognize their emotions and respond with patience and empathy creates a positive and inclusive learning atmosphere.

A teacher with high emotional intelligence can sense when a student is struggling, feeling anxious, or losing motivation. Instead of dismissing these emotions, they take the time to understand the student's perspective and provide support. This could be as simple as offering encouragement, giving extra time for assignments, or having a one-on-one conversation to address concerns. When students feel emotionally supported, they are more likely to stay engaged and motivated in their studies.

Moreover, emotionally intelligent teachers lead by example. They demonstrate qualities like patience, kindness, and resilience, which students, in turn, learn and adopt. By managing their own emotions well, teachers create an environment of mutual respect and understanding, making learning a more fulfilling experience.

A Story: The Teacher Who Saw Beyond Academics

In a bustling city school, there was a student named Aryan who, despite being intelligent, struggled with concentration and motivation. Most teachers labeled him as 'distracted' and 'uninterested,' but one teacher, Mr. Mehta, took a different approach. Instead of reprimanding him, he observed Aryan closely and discovered that the student had a deep passion for storytelling and creative writing. However, since most subjects focused on rigid structures and memorization, Aryan felt disconnected.

Instead of forcing Aryan to conform, Mr. Mehta encouraged him to express his thoughts through writing. He allowed him to present history lessons as stories and explain scientific concepts through creative essays. Slowly, Aryan's grades improved, but more importantly, his confidence and love for learning grew. Years later, Aryan became a successful author, and in interviews, he always credited Mr. Mehta as the teacher who saw his potential when others didn't.

This story highlights the importance of emotional intelligence in teaching. Every student learns differently, and a teacher's role is not just to teach subjects but to understand students as individuals. A great teacher sees beyond grades and textbooks—they see the dreams, fears, and potential hidden within each student and nurture it in a way that helps them grow into confident and capable individuals.

Teaching Beyond Grades: Inspiring a Love for Learning

A teacher's greatest achievement is not producing students with high marks but fostering a lifelong love for learning. In many education systems, students are often taught to study for grades rather than for knowledge. While examinations are an important measure of academic progress, they should not become the sole focus of education. The true goal of teaching should be to help students develop curiosity, critical thinking, and a desire to explore knowledge beyond what is required for exams.

A student who learns merely to pass tests may forget information after the exams, but a student who learns out of genuine curiosity retains knowledge for life. Great teachers understand this difference and create an environment where students feel excited about learning, rather than pressured to score high. When teachers encourage open discussions, practical applications, and creative thinking, they transform the learning process into a journey rather than a task.

The Power of Curiosity and Independent Thinking

One of the best qualities a teacher can cultivate in students is curiosity. The greatest discoveries and innovations in history have come from people who were curious about the world and dared to ask questions. Instead of simply delivering information, teachers should encourage students to wonder why things work the way they do, how different concepts connect, and what real-world problems can be solved using their knowledge.

Independent thinking is another crucial skill that teachers can nurture. Instead of expecting students to memorize answers, teachers should challenge them to think critically. For example, in a history class, rather than just memorizing dates and events, students could analyze why historical events happened and what lessons can be learned from them. In science, instead of just reading formulas, students could be encouraged to conduct experiments and draw their own conclusions. These approaches make learning more meaningful and enjoyable.

The Role of Storytelling and Real-Life Examples in Teaching

One of the most effective ways to make learning engaging is through storytelling. Throughout history, knowledge has been passed down through stories, which make complex ideas easier to understand and remember. A great teacher knows how to bring lessons to life by weaving them into stories that capture students' imaginations. For instance, instead of explaining abstract mathematical concepts in isolation, a teacher could use real-world examples, such as how mathematicians like Ramanujan solved problems that seemed impossible in their time.

Real-life examples also make education more relevant. When students see how their lessons apply to the world around them, they become more interested in learning. For example, a physics teacher explaining gravity could connect the lesson to space travel and how astronauts experience microgravity. A business studies teacher could use real companies as case studies, helping students understand how business strategies work in reality. The more relatable and engaging a lesson is, the more likely students are to remember it.

A Story: The Teacher Who Made Learning Come Alive

In a small village school, students struggled to stay engaged in their lessons. Most of them memorized answers without understanding the concepts. One day, a new teacher, Mr. Ramesh, joined the school. Instead of following traditional methods, he started using storytelling and hands-on experiments to teach subjects. In a history lesson, he turned the classroom into a courtroom, where students acted as historical figures debating decisions that shaped the world. In science, he took students outside to conduct real experiments rather than just reading theories from books.

Gradually, the students who once found learning dull began to participate eagerly. They started asking more questions, exploring topics on their own, and most importantly, enjoying the process of learning. Years later, many of those students recalled how Mr. Ramesh changed their perspective on education—not by forcing them to study, but by making them love learning.

This story is a reminder that education is most effective when it is engaging, relevant, and enjoyable. Teachers have the power to shape how students view learning, not just for their school years, but for their entire lives.

The Future of Teaching: Adapting to a Changing World

As the world continues to evolve at a rapid pace, so must the education system and the role of teachers within it. The rise of technology, changing career landscapes, and new learning methodologies require teachers to constantly adapt and innovate. Traditional classroom methods, which focused on passive learning and memorization, are giving way to interactive, student-centered education. The future of teaching is not about simply delivering lectures but about creating an engaging learning experience that prepares students for real-world challenges.

To stay relevant, teachers must embrace lifelong learning themselves. Just as students are expected to keep up with evolving knowledge, educators must continuously upgrade their skills. This means staying updated with the latest educational tools, integrating technology into lessons, and adopting modern teaching strategies that cater to different learning styles. Whether it is through digital learning platforms, gamification of lessons, or personalized mentoring, the role of teachers is expanding beyond traditional boundaries.

Empowering Teachers: How We Can Support Them

For teachers to thrive in their evolving roles, they need adequate support from educational institutions, policymakers, and society as a whole. One of the most crucial aspects is reducing the administrative burden placed on teachers. Many educators spend a significant amount of time on paperwork and bureaucratic tasks, taking away valuable hours that could be dedicated to student interaction and lesson planning. Streamlining these processes and providing assistive technologies can help teachers focus on what truly matters—teaching and mentoring.

Professional development programs are also essential. Governments and schools should provide teachers with regular training in new teaching methods, classroom management strategies, and subject advancements. This will not only enhance their skills but also keep them motivated and inspired to continue making a difference.

Another critical factor is ensuring that teachers are financially and socially respected. In many countries, teachers are among the most respected professionals, enjoying high salaries and strong societal recognition. India needs to further strengthen its commitment to educators by improving salary structures, offering career growth opportunities, and recognizing outstanding contributions in the field of education. A society that values its teachers ultimately nurtures a more educated and prosperous generation.

A Vision for the Future: Teachers as Nation-Builders

Teachers are more than just educators; they are nation-builders. Every successful scientist, entrepreneur, doctor, engineer, and artist owes a part of their journey to the teachers who guided them. By empowering teachers, we invest in the future of our country. Schools should not just be institutions of academic learning but hubs of creativity, critical thinking, and character development. Teachers, when given the right tools and recognition, can shape the future of society in ways no other profession can.

As Dr. Sarvepalli Radhakrishnan, former President of India and a distinguished educator, once said, 'Teachers should be the best minds in the country.' By ensuring that our educators are well-equipped, motivated, and valued, we can build an education system that does not just produce graduates but cultivates visionaries, leaders, and problem-solvers for the world.

The role of teachers is irreplaceable. While technology can enhance learning, it is the human touch, the mentorship, and the guidance of a teacher that truly transforms lives. As we move forward, let us strive to create an environment where teachers are not just instructors but lifelong mentors who shape the minds of future generations.

CHAPTER 7

The Role of Students – Beyond Just Learners

Let's talk, just you and me. Forget the textbooks for a moment. Forget the pressure of exams and grades. I want you to really think about something—what does it mean to be a student? Is it just about sitting in a classroom, listening to lectures, memorizing facts, and scoring marks? Or is it something more?

Being a student isn't just about attending school or college. It's about growing, questioning, and shaping your mind. It's about preparing for life, not just for a job. The world is full of people who have degrees but no real understanding. Don't just be someone who learns for an exam—be someone who learns for life.

Education Is More Than Just Grades and Exams

I know what you might be thinking—'But marks matter! Exams decide my future!' And yes, they do play a role. But let me tell you something important—marks are not everything. If you only study to pass exams, you are missing the true purpose of learning. The real goal of education is not just to get a certificate; it is to understand the world, solve problems, and develop the skills that will help you no matter what career you choose.

Think about some of the greatest minds in history—Albert Einstein, Dr. A.P.J. Abdul Kalam, Steve Jobs. Do you think they succeeded just because they scored high in exams? No. They succeeded because they were curious. They asked questions. They explored beyond the syllabus. If you want to truly become educated, you must do the same. Question what you learn. Try to apply it in real life. Understand, don't just memorize.

Taking Charge of Your Own Learning

Here's a truth that most students don't realize—you are responsible for your own learning. Teachers, parents, and schools can guide you, but at the end of the day, it's up to you. If you sit in class waiting for knowledge to be handed to you, you will never grow beyond what is written in your textbooks. But if you take charge—if you read beyond the syllabus, explore new ideas, and challenge yourself—you will develop a mind that is sharp, independent, and unstoppable.

You live in a time where information is at your fingertips. You can learn anything—science, business, coding, music, art—without waiting for someone to teach you. If you truly want to grow, start learning beyond what is expected. Take a course online, read books outside your syllabus, experiment with new skills. The most successful people are those who never stop learning, no matter where they are in life.

So, I ask you—what kind of student do you want to be? One who follows the system blindly, or one who uses education as a tool to build a future full of opportunities? The choice is yours, but remember—learning is not a task, it's an adventure. And the best students are the ones who enjoy the journey.

Embracing a Growth Mindset: Learning from Mistakes

Let me tell you something that most students don't realize—failure is not the opposite of success; it's part of success. Many of us are afraid of making mistakes because we think failure means we are not good enough. But the truth is, every great mind that changed the world failed at some point. The difference is, they didn't give up—they learned from it.

Think about Thomas Edison. He failed thousands of times before he finally created the light bulb. Imagine if he had given up after the first few failures—our world would be very different today. The same applies to you. If you fail a test, if you struggle with a subject, if you make mistakes—it doesn't mean you're not smart. It means you're learning. The only real failure is when you stop trying.

This is called having a 'growth mindset'—the belief that intelligence and abilities can be developed with effort and persistence. Instead of saying, 'I'm bad at math,' say, 'I haven't mastered it yet, but I will.' Instead of thinking, 'I can't do this,' tell yourself, 'I just need to practice more.' The way you talk to yourself shapes your learning journey. A student with a growth mindset sees challenges as opportunities, not obstacles.

The Power of Self-Discipline and Consistency

Here's a secret—talent alone is not enough. The students who succeed are not always the smartest ones, but the ones who show up every day, who put in the effort, who stay disciplined. Self-discipline is what separates those who achieve their dreams from those who give up too soon.

Imagine you want to build muscles. If you go to the gym once a month and lift heavy weights for hours, will you get stronger? No. But if you exercise a little bit every day, you'll see results. Learning works the same way. Studying for 10 hours before an exam won't help as much as studying for one hour every day. Consistency is the real game-changer.

Discipline is also about managing distractions. Social media, video games, and endless entertainment can steal hours from your day without you even noticing. I'm not saying you shouldn't enjoy your free time, but learn to control it. Set goals, manage your time wisely, and make studying a habit. The students who learn this early become unstoppable in life.

Real Education Happens Outside the Classroom

If you think education is only about what happens inside a classroom, let me challenge that idea. Some of the most valuable lessons you'll ever learn will come from experiences outside of school. Traveling, meeting new people, taking up hobbies, working on projects—these are all forms of education too.

Think about a student who only studies from books and another who also participates in debates, joins clubs, and works on creative projects. Who do you think will have a better understanding of the world? Who will be more confident, better at problem-solving, and ready for the future? The one who learns beyond books.

So step outside your comfort zone. Try new things. Volunteer, explore, ask questions, and seek experiences that challenge you. Education is not just about marks—it's about preparing for life.

At the end of the day, your education is in your hands. Whether you just go through the system or truly take control of your learning—that's up to you.

Taking Responsibility for Your Own Learning

Let's be honest—no one can force you to learn. Your teachers can teach, your parents can encourage you, but in the end, your education is in your hands. You are the one who decides whether to truly understand something or just memorize it for an exam. You are the one who chooses whether to challenge yourself or take the easy way out. If you want to succeed—not just in school, but in life—you must take responsibility for your own learning.

Think of your education like a journey. No one else can walk it for you. The students who take responsibility for their learning don't wait for teachers to spoon-feed them information. They ask questions, they explore beyond the syllabus, and they actively seek knowledge. If you start seeing learning as something you do for yourself—not for grades, not for parents, not for teachers—you will begin to enjoy it more.

How to Stay Motivated Even When Studies Feel Overwhelming

We all have moments when studying feels like a burden. There are days when you just don't feel like opening a book, when assignments pile up, and when everything seems too difficult. It's normal. But what separates successful students from others is how they deal with those moments.

The secret to staying motivated is simple: remind yourself why you are learning. What is your goal? What excites you? If you don't have an answer, find one. It doesn't have to be a big dream—it could be as simple as wanting to improve in a subject you struggle with, wanting to learn a new skill, or wanting to prove to yourself that you can do better.

Another trick to staying motivated is breaking things into small steps. Don't think about studying for 5 hours— just start with 20 minutes. Don't think about completing an entire syllabus—just focus on understanding one topic. Motivation grows when you take action, even if it's small.

And here's something important—don't be afraid to ask for help. If you're stuck on something, reach out to teachers, classmates, or even online resources. Learning is not about struggling alone; it's about finding the best way forward.

The Value of Teamwork and Learning from Others

You don't have to do it all alone. Some of the best learning happens through discussions, debates, and collaboration. Think about it—when you try to explain something to a friend, you understand it better yourself. When you work on projects as a team, you get exposed to different ideas and perspectives. The most successful people in the world didn't succeed alone; they learned from others, worked with others, and grew together.

So, take part in group discussions. Join study groups. Challenge your classmates with interesting questions. If you struggle in a subject, find a friend who understands it well and learn from them. And if you are good at something, teach others—it will make you even better.

Education is not a competition; it's a journey. The more you share knowledge, the more you grow. So don't just be a student—be a learner, a thinker, a teammate, and most importantly, someone who is excited about discovering new things every day.

Balancing Studies with Personal Growth

Let's be clear—studying is important. But if all you do is memorize books and chase grades, you are missing out on something bigger. Education is not just about what happens inside the classroom. It's also about how you grow as a person, how you develop skills that will help you in real life, and how you prepare for challenges beyond exams.

Some students believe that getting top marks guarantees success. But think about this—what happens when two people with the same qualifications apply for a job? The one who stands out is the one with confidence, problem-solving skills, and the ability to communicate effectively. Your grades can open doors, but it is your personality, skills, and mindset that will determine how far you go.

Developing Skills That Go Beyond Academics

Apart from studying, every student should focus on building skills that will help them in the real world. Communication is one of the most important skills you can develop. Whether you are speaking in front of a class, explaining an idea, or attending an interview, the way you express your thoughts matters. Practice speaking confidently, learn how to listen actively, and work on improving your writing skills.

Leadership is another skill that can set you apart. You don't have to be the head of a group to be a leader—you just need to take responsibility, help others, and be proactive. Whether it's organizing a school event, mentoring a junior student, or taking the initiative in a class project, every small step builds leadership qualities.

Problem-solving is a skill that will help you in every stage of life. Instead of avoiding challenges, learn to analyze problems, find solutions, and think creatively. Successful people are not the ones who never face problems; they are the ones who know how to deal with them.

Stepping Out of Your Comfort Zone

Many students stay within their comfort zones because they fear failure or embarrassment. But growth happens when you push yourself beyond what feels easy. Join a competition even if you are nervous. Speak up in class even if you are shy. Try something new, whether it's a sport, a creative hobby, or an online course. Every time you challenge yourself, you become stronger and more confident.

Remember, education is not just about passing exams—it's about preparing yourself for life. The best students are not just the ones who score well; they are the ones who learn, grow, and challenge themselves to be better every day.

Creating a Vision for Your Future

Let's talk about your future. Not just about which career you will choose, but about the kind of person you want to become. What do you see yourself doing five years from now? Ten years from now? If you don't have an answer yet, that's okay. But start thinking about it. The choices you make today will shape the person you become tomorrow.

Success doesn't happen overnight. It starts with small steps—developing good habits, making the most of opportunities, and always being ready to learn. The most successful people are not the ones who always knew exactly what they wanted. They are the ones who stayed open to learning, kept improving, and adapted to new challenges.

Resilience: Learning to Bounce Back from Failures

Life will not always go the way you planned. You will face setbacks, disappointments, and moments of self-doubt. But here's something important to remember—your failures do not define you. How you respond to them does.

Think about this—every great person you admire has failed at some point. But they didn't let failure stop them. Instead, they learned from it and kept going. If you get a bad grade, don't be discouraged—figure out what went wrong and improve. If you don't succeed at something on the first try, don't give up—try again with a new approach. The ability to bounce back and keep moving forward is one of the most powerful skills you can develop.

Becoming a Lifelong Learner

School will end one day, but learning never should. The world is changing every day, and the people who succeed are the ones who never stop learning. Read books, explore new ideas, challenge yourself, and stay curious. Education is not just about passing exams—it's about growing, evolving, and making your mark on the world.

So as you move forward, don't just aim to be a good student. Aim to be a great learner. Someone who is always hungry for knowledge, always ready to improve, and always willing to take on new challenges. Because at the end of the day, education is not just about where you go—it's about who you become.

CHAPTER 8

The Challenges Faced by Students in the Learning Process

Being a student is not easy. Every day, students face academic pressure, expectations from parents and teachers, competition with peers, and the constant challenge of balancing studies with personal life. While education is meant to be an enriching experience, for many students, it becomes a source of stress and anxiety. But why does this happen? And how can we make learning a healthier and more fulfilling journey?

I would like to share a recent incident from my classroom. It happened right after a board exam. One of my students, a boy who usually keeps his emotions bottled up, broke down into tears. The exam time had ended, and a few questions were left unanswered. He was trembling, struggling to control his emotions, and his tears weren't just about those incomplete answers. They carried the weight of all the silent fears, pressures, and self-doubts that had been building up inside him.

In that moment, I didn't correct him or offer advice about time management. I didn't talk about marks or syllabus completion. Instead, I simply hugged him. I told him gently, "It's okay." Those two words — so simple, yet so powerful — gave him the space to breathe. His sobs gradually eased. To lighten the moment, I invited him to have lunch with me, not as his teacher, but as someone who cared more about him than about his performance.

This small interaction made me reflect on a much larger reality — one that plays out in classrooms across the country. Every year, countless students cry silently before exams, their hearts gripped with fear. Some break down just minutes before they enter the examination hall. With trembling hands, they whisper to themselves or to their friends, "What will we do? We aren't fully prepared." That fear is not always because they didn't study — it's often because they carry an invisible burden of expectations, comparisons, and the belief that their worth depends entirely on a score.

As educators and parents, we need to pause and ask ourselves: Are we preparing our children for exams, or are we preparing them for life?

"Behind every trembling hand holding a pen is a heart that simply wants to be understood."

Exams are undoubtedly important, but they should not become a source of trauma. Our role is not just to teach subjects, but to teach resilience, self-belief, and emotional strength. Children need to know that it is okay to make mistakes, to forget answers, and to feel nervous — these are all part of learning and growing. More importantly, they need to know that our love, respect, and pride in them do not hinge on perfect marks.

So, what can we do — as teachers, as parents — to truly support our children?

Create a safe space: Before exams, talk to them, not about marks, but about their feelings. Let them express their fears without judgment.

Focus on process, not just results: Teach them to break their preparation into small, manageable steps. Celebrate the effort, not just the outcome.

Normalize mistakes: Share your own stories of failure and how you overcame them. Let them know that even the most successful people have stumbled many times.

Remind them of their worth: Constantly reinforce the message that their value as a person is far greater than any exam score could ever show.

Be present after the exam: Regardless of the result, be there to listen, comfort, and guide — showing them that every experience, whether success or failure, has something to teach.

When we shift our focus from performance to progress, from marks to mindset, we not only reduce exam stress but also raise emotionally healthier, more confident children. Exams will come and go, but the life lessons we teach in these moments of vulnerability — those stay forever.

The truth is, no two students learn the same way. Some grasp concepts quickly, while others need more time. Some excel in science, while others shine in art. Despite these differences, the education system often expects all students to perform at the same level, using the same methods. This creates frustration, self-doubt, and unnecessary pressure. Instead of celebrating individual learning styles, many students feel they are constantly being measured by grades alone.

The Biggest Challenges Students Face

Academic Pressure and High Expectations

One of the most common struggles students face is the pressure to perform well in exams. Marks often become the primary measure of intelligence, leading students to focus on memorization rather than true understanding. When learning becomes a race for grades, curiosity and creativity suffer.

Distractions in the Digital Age

Technology has opened endless learning opportunities, but it has also brought distractions. Social media, gaming, and constant notifications make it difficult for students to focus. Many students struggle with time management because their study hours are interrupted by digital distractions.

Mental Stress and Anxiety

Fear of failure, comparison with others, and an overloaded schedule take a toll on students' mental health. Many students feel alone in their struggles because mental health is rarely discussed openly. Anxiety and stress can make learning more difficult and lead to a loss of confidence.

Creating a Supportive Learning Environment

Schools, parents, and society play a crucial role in making education a positive experience. Instead of just focusing on results, we must encourage effort, progress, and well-being. Teachers should understand that every student learns at their own pace. Parents should focus on emotional support rather than just expectations. And students should be encouraged to ask for help without fear of judgment.

The learning process is different for everyone, and challenges are part of growth. By acknowledging and addressing these struggles, we can create an education system that values learning, creativity, and mental well-being as much as it values academic achievement.

Different Students, Different Challenges

Not all students face the same challenges. While some struggle with academic pressure, others deal with emotional stress, economic difficulties, or social issues. Understanding that every student's journey is unique is the first step toward finding solutions. By recognizing these struggles, we can create a more inclusive and supportive learning environment.

Balancing Studies with Extracurricular Activities and Personal Interests

Many students today are not just expected to perform well in academics but also to participate in extracurricular activities like sports, music, or debates. While these activities are valuable for overall development, they also add to the workload, leaving students feeling exhausted and overwhelmed.

The key to balancing academics and extracurriculars is time management. Students must learn to prioritize tasks, create schedules, and set realistic goals. Instead of trying to do everything at once, they should focus on what truly matters to them. Schools and parents should also recognize that learning happens outside the classroom too and support students in exploring their passions.

Overcoming Challenges with the Right Mindset and Support

Every challenge, whether academic, social, or personal, has a solution. The most successful students are not those who never face difficulties, but those who learn how to overcome them. Developing a growth mindset—where failures are seen as learning experiences rather than obstacles—helps students stay motivated and resilient.

Seeking help when needed is also important. Many students hesitate to ask questions in class or discuss their struggles with teachers and parents. However, open communication and a strong support system can make a huge difference in overcoming challenges. Schools should create a culture where students feel comfortable seeking guidance without fear of judgment.

At the end of the day, every student has the potential to succeed. With the right mindset, proper support, and a willingness to adapt, any obstacle can be turned into an opportunity for growth.

The Impact of Peer Pressure and Societal Expectations

Every student, at some point, feels the pressure of fitting in. Whether it's about performing well in academics, choosing a career path that society approves of, or simply meeting the expectations of friends and family, peer pressure is real. Many students find themselves making decisions based on what others think rather than what they truly want.

The truth is, no two students are the same. Everyone has different strengths, interests, and dreams. Trying to live up to someone else's expectations can lead to frustration, anxiety, and a loss of self-identity. The best way to overcome peer pressure is to be confident in your own journey. Instead of following the crowd, take time to discover what you are truly passionate about. Success is not about doing what others expect—it's about finding what fulfills you.

The Fear of Failure and Its Effect on Learning

One of the biggest reasons students struggle with learning is the fear of failure. The education system often makes students believe that failing an exam or scoring low marks is a sign of weakness. However, failure is not the end—it is a step toward growth.

Think about some of the greatest minds in history—Thomas Edison, Albert Einstein, Dr. A.P.J. Abdul Kalam. They all faced failures, but they never gave up. Instead of seeing failure as a roadblock, they used it as a lesson to improve and move forward. Students who adopt this mindset become more resilient and confident in their learning abilities.

How to Stay Motivated and Focused Despite Pressure

Staying motivated in a world full of distractions and pressure is not easy, but it is possible. One of the best ways to stay focused is to set small, achievable goals. Instead of worrying about the final exam, break your studies into daily or weekly tasks. Completing small goals gives you a sense of achievement and keeps you motivated.

Another effective strategy is to surround yourself with positive influences. Spend time with people who encourage and inspire you. If you are struggling, talk to a teacher, mentor, or friend who can guide you. Remember, you are not alone in this journey—everyone faces challenges, but those who push through them come out stronger.

At the end of the day, learning is not just about exams or competition—it is about growth. Stay curious, stay determined, and believe in yourself. Your journey is unique, and as long as you keep moving forward, you are on the right path.

Overcoming Lack of Motivation and Boredom in Learning

One of the biggest struggles students face is a lack of motivation. Studying can often feel repetitive and uninteresting, especially when subjects are taught in a way that doesn't spark curiosity. Many students lose interest because they don't see how their studies relate to real life or future goals.

The key to overcoming boredom is to find personal meaning in what you learn. Instead of just memorizing facts, try to connect them to something interesting. For example, if you're learning about history, imagine yourself as part of the event. If you're studying math, explore how it applies to real-world problems. Learning is much more engaging when you see its relevance.

Developing Better Concentration and Study Habits

In today's world of distractions, focusing on studies can be difficult. Many students struggle with concentration because of social media, noise, or a lack of effective study techniques. However, concentration is a skill that can be developed with practice.

One effective method is the 'Pomodoro Technique'—studying for 25 minutes and then taking a 5-minute break. This helps keep the brain fresh and focused. Another tip is to create a dedicated study space, free from distractions. Keeping your phone away while studying and using productivity apps can also help improve focus.

A good study habit is not just about long hours—it's about smart learning. Instead of cramming, revise regularly. Use techniques like mind maps, flashcards, and teaching concepts to others. The more interactive your study methods, the better you retain information.

The Role of Schools and Teachers in Making Learning Engaging

Students are not the only ones responsible for making learning interesting—schools and teachers also play a huge role. Traditional rote learning, where students memorize without understanding, often kills curiosity. Instead, teachers should focus on interactive learning, real-world applications, and discussions that encourage critical thinking.

Education should not just be about textbooks. Schools should integrate activities like debates, group projects, hands-on experiments, and storytelling to make lessons more engaging. When students feel actively involved in the learning process, they develop a natural interest in education.

At the end of the day, learning should not feel like a burden—it should feel like an adventure. The more we make education engaging, the more students will develop a lifelong love for learning.

Emotional Resilience and Mental Well-Being in Education

Education is not just about academics—it is also about building emotional strength. Many students struggle with stress, self-doubt, and the fear of failure. In a competitive environment, it is easy to feel overwhelmed, but emotional resilience can help students navigate these challenges.

Resilience means being able to bounce back from failures, stay motivated during tough times, and maintain a positive mindset despite difficulties. Students who develop resilience are more likely to face challenges with confidence rather than fear.

Developing a Positive Mindset Despite Setbacks

Setbacks are a part of learning. Every student faces moments when they struggle with a subject, score lower than expected, or feel discouraged. But setbacks do not define success—how students respond to them does. Instead of seeing failures as roadblocks, students should view them as opportunities to improve.

A positive mindset starts with self-talk. Instead of saying, 'I'm not good at this,' students should say, 'I am still learning, and I will get better.' Small changes in how we think can make a huge difference in motivation and confidence.

Seeking help when needed is also important. Whether it's talking to a teacher, a parent, or a friend, discussing challenges openly can provide support and solutions. No student has to go through their struggles alone.

Every student's journey is unique, and challenges are a natural part of growth. The most successful people in the world did not succeed because they never failed—they succeeded because they never gave up. Learning is a lifelong process, and the obstacles faced today will shape the strengths of tomorrow.

Education is not just about grades or achievements—it is about becoming a stronger, wiser, and more capable individual. Keep learning, keep growing, and remember that every challenge you overcome brings you one step closer to success.

CHAPTER 9

From Reels to Real Learning – Navigating Social Media for Growth

It was a pleasant evening, and I had stepped out for a walk. I saw my neighbour's son, a little boy, was sitting on the floor of their veranda. His small hands were wrapped around a phone almost as big as his face. His eyes were wide, fixed on the screen as he scrolled through a series of reels — bright colours flashing rapidly, catchy music playing in the background. His face showed a kind of hypnotic focus, the kind you might expect from an adult handling a complex task — but here it was, mirrored on the innocent face of a child.

His mother called him from inside the house, but he didn't respond. She called again, louder this time. He stirred slightly but kept his gaze on the screen. A group of children were playing just outside — laughing, running, and calling out to each other — but the boy remained still, his thumbs swiping mechanically.

I sat down next to him and gently asked, "What are you watching?"

"LOOK! A MAN IS BITING A DOG," he laughed out loud while showing it to me.

"Why don't you go play with your friends?" I suggested.

He shrugged. "This is better."

Just then, one of the kids from the group shouted his name, inviting him to join the game. He ignored it. His eyes never left the screen. His little fingers kept swiping, drawn to the next burst of stimulation.

It struck me how this is becoming an increasingly common sight. Children, barely able to read or write, are glued to the addictive cycle of social media. But it's not their fault. How can it be? The devices are handed to them to keep them occupied. Parents, caught up in their own busy lives, often find it easier to calm a restless child with a phone than to engage them in conversation or play. Algorithms designed to capture attention ensure that once a child starts swiping, it's almost impossible to stop.

It's not just about distraction — it's about what they're missing. That boy wasn't just ignoring play; he was unknowingly turning away from the process of learning itself. The natural curiosity that drives children to explore, ask questions, and engage with the world was being replaced by passive consumption of fleeting content.

This isn't a failure of the child. It's a reflection of the environment we've created — one where convenience often outweighs connection, and stimulation replaces curiosity. The challenge before us is not to blame children for being drawn to screens but to ask ourselves how we can create a world where real learning — through play, conversation, and exploration — feels more rewarding than the next swipe.

Social media has become a defining force in modern life. Platforms like TikTok, Instagram, and YouTube have reshaped how we communicate, learn, and entertain ourselves. The staggering statistics reflect this shift: over 4.5 billion people actively use social media globally, with the average person spending nearly 2.5 hours per day on these platforms. But for younger audiences—high school and college students—the engagement levels are even higher. A 2023 report by DataReportal revealed that teens spend an average of 4.8 hours daily scrolling through social media feeds.

But why is it so hard to stop? Why does a quick five-minute break to check Instagram Reels or YouTube Shorts often spiral into a two-hour binge? The answer lies deep within the brain's reward system and the way social media platforms have mastered the art of capturing and monetizing attention.

The Dopamine Loop – Why Scrolling Feels So Good

At the heart of social media addiction is a powerful chemical called dopamine. Dopamine is the brain's "feel-good" neurotransmitter—it's released whenever you experience something pleasurable, such as eating chocolate, winning a game, or hearing a funny joke. Social media platforms have engineered their designs to trigger this chemical release repeatedly and consistently.

Every time you scroll and encounter a funny meme, a motivational quote, or a visually stunning travel video, your brain gives you a small hit of dopamine. This creates a cycle:

1. You watch a video → Dopamine hit → You feel good
2. Your brain craves more dopamine → You keep scrolling
3. The loop repeats—again and again

This is why it's so easy to lose track of time. The brain starts associating social media with pleasure, and the craving for that quick hit of dopamine overrides your ability to stop. Platforms like YouTube and Instagram are designed to reinforce this loop using algorithms that analyse your behaviour, preferences, and engagement patterns.

According to Tristan Harris, former Google ethicist and founder of the Center for Humane Technology:

"If you are not paying for the product, you are the product."

The Role of Algorithms – How They Trap You

Social media platforms use sophisticated algorithms to curate your feed. These algorithms track everything:

- What you like
- What you comment on

- How long you linger on a post
- What you share
- Even how quickly you scroll

The algorithm then creates a personalized feed designed to maximize your engagement. If you liked a video about workout routines, the algorithm will serve you more fitness content. If you clicked on a funny cat video, expect more cute animal clips. The goal is simple: keep you hooked.

A 2022 study by The Journal of Behavioural Addictions found that algorithm-driven content increased user engagement by 67% compared to non-algorithmic content. In other words, when platforms actively control what you see, you're more likely to keep watching.

The Attention Span Crisis

Our brains are not equipped to handle this constant influx of fast-paced content. Research confirms that social media has contributed to a significant decline in attention spans over the last two decades.

A 2022 study by Microsoft found that the average human attention span has dropped from 12 seconds in 2000 to just 8 seconds—shorter than the attention span of a goldfish.

Short-form content, like YouTube Shorts and Instagram Reels, reinforces this problem by training the brain to expect quick rewards. If a video doesn't capture your attention within the first 3 seconds, you're likely to scroll away. This conditioning erodes the brain's ability to focus on longer, more complex tasks—like reading a book or studying for an exam.

Consider the case of Meera, a high school junior:

"I used to love reading novels," Meera says. "But now, I can't focus for more than a few minutes. Even when I try to read, my mind keeps drifting, and I get the urge to check my phone."

Instant Gratification vs. Deep Work

The concept of "deep work" was introduced by author and productivity expert Cal Newport. Deep work refers to the ability to focus intensely on a cognitively demanding task without distraction. It's the mental state where you engage in complex problem-solving, creative thinking, and long-term goal setting.

But deep work is increasingly rare. When the brain becomes accustomed to short, high-reward bursts of dopamine from social media, it struggles to engage in deeper, more sustained mental effort. Newport argues that this shift is one of the biggest threats to learning and personal development in the modern age.

"Focus is the new IQ," Newport states. "In a world where attention is constantly being fragmented, those who can master focus will have a significant competitive advantage."

The Psychological Design of Social Media

Social media platforms don't just exploit dopamine—they use psychological design tricks to deepen the addiction.

- Infinite Scroll: Platforms like YouTube Shorts and Instagram use an endless feed that refreshes automatically.
- Notifications: The red badge or chime triggers a sense of urgency and anticipation, prompting you to check the app even when you weren't planning to.
- Likes and Comments: Positive social feedback (likes, comments, shares) provides a powerful sense of validation, reinforcing the craving for more interaction.

Understanding the Mechanism – The First Step to Taking Control

The first step to reclaiming control over your attention is understanding how social media platforms are designed to manipulate your brain's reward system. When you realize that the endless scroll isn't a coincidence—but a calculated feature designed to hijack your attention—you can begin to resist it.

Social media's influence on the brain extends beyond mere distraction—it's fundamentally altering how we think, process information, and retain knowledge. While platforms like Instagram Reels, and YouTube Shorts provide quick bursts of entertainment and information, their long-term effects on cognitive function, emotional well-being, and learning capabilities are profound and often damaging.

What makes short-form content so appealing is exactly what makes it harmful for deep learning: speed, simplicity, and instant gratification. The very structure of these platforms encourages shallow thinking and conditions the brain to avoid sustained mental effort. Over time, this weakens critical cognitive functions, diminishes emotional regulation, and reshapes how the brain processes information.

1. Reduced Focus and Cognitive Endurance

Deep learning requires focused attention over extended periods. When you study a complex math problem, analyze a piece of literature, or write a research paper, your brain engages in a state of what psychologist Mihaly Csikszentmihalyi calls "flow"—a mental state where concentration deepens, creativity emerges, and information is processed at a high level.

However, short-form content directly undermines this ability. The rapid, fragmented nature of Reels conditions the brain to expect quick rewards and immediate stimulation. If a video doesn't hook the viewer in the first three seconds, most users will swipe away. This repeated pattern reshapes the brain's ability to sustain attention.

A 2021 study by the University of California, Irvine found that the average worker switches between tasks every three minutes and five seconds—a 50% decline in sustained attention compared to just a decade earlier. The study linked this shift directly to the rise of social media and the increasing consumption of short-form content.

2. Superficial Learning and Reduced Retention

Psychologist John Sweller introduced the concept of Cognitive Load Theory—which explains how the brain processes information. When information is presented too quickly or without proper structure, the brain struggles to transfer it into long-term memory. Short-form content overloads the brain with fragmented facts, making it harder to consolidate that knowledge into a cohesive understanding.

A 2022 study published in the journal Memory & Cognition confirmed that short-form content improves recall but reduces comprehension. Participants could remember details from a short video but struggled to apply that knowledge in new contexts or analyze it critically.

3. Emotional Instability and Mental Health Issues

Beyond cognitive effects, short-form content also influences emotional well-being. Social media platforms thrive on engagement, and one of the most effective ways to boost engagement is through emotional stimulation—whether positive or negative.

Algorithms prioritize emotionally charged content because it triggers stronger reactions:

- Outrage
- Envy
- Admiration
- Humor
- Shock

This creates a toxic emotional rollercoaster. A user might see a heartwarming video about a rescue dog, followed immediately by a distressing news clip, followed by an influencer flaunting luxury vacations. This rapid emotional shifting destabilizes emotional regulation and increases feelings of anxiety, inadequacy, and depression.

A 2021 study by the Royal Society for Public Health found that social media—especially platforms centered around visual content like Instagram—correlates with increased rates of:

Anxiety (+70%)

Depression (+68%)

Poor sleep quality (+65%)

Negative body image (+60%)

Psychologist Dr. Jean Twenge, author of iGen, points to the rise of social media as a major driver behind increased rates of teen depression and anxiety:

"Social media platforms create a false sense of social comparison—people present curated versions of their lives that are unattainable. This fuels feelings of inadequacy and alienation among teens."

The Positive Side – How to Use Social Media for Learning

While the negative effects of social media on learning are well-documented, it's important to recognize that social media itself isn't inherently bad. The same platforms that foster addiction, superficial thinking, and emotional instability also hold enormous potential for learning, skill development, and personal growth—if used strategically.

Social media is a double-edged sword. On one hand, it conditions the brain for quick rewards and reduces attention spans. On the other hand, it offers access to vast amounts of information, global perspectives, and innovative learning methods. The key lies not in rejecting social media altogether but in shifting from passive consumption to active engagement.

1. Curated Learning – Turning Algorithms to Your Advantage

The algorithms that drive engagement on social media can also be leveraged to support learning—if you feed them the right signals. Social media platforms are designed to give you more of what you engage with. If you spend most of your time watching prank videos, your feed will be filled with similar content. But if you actively seek out educational content, the algorithm will begin to serve you more of it.

2. Micro-Learning – The Power of Short Bursts

Short-form content is not inherently harmful; the problem lies in how it's used. When consumed passively, it becomes a source of distraction. But when used strategically, short-form content can enhance memory retention and improve cognitive performance through a technique called spaced repetition.

Educational psychologist Dr. Barbara Oakley explains:

"The brain retains information better when it's introduced in short, manageable bursts over time. Social media, when used with intention, can provide the perfect format for spaced repetition."

3. Skill-Based Learning – Expanding Beyond Traditional Education

Social media platforms aren't just for theoretical learning—they're also hubs for skill development. From coding and cooking to fitness and photography, short-form content allows users to explore new skills and hobbies beyond the traditional classroom setting.

Examples:

- A student interested in photography can follow professional photographers for editing tips and shooting techniques.
- Aspiring coders can watch quick Python coding tutorials on YouTube Shorts.
- Fitness enthusiasts can access workout routines tailored to specific goals.

4. Community and Collaboration – Learning Together

One of social media's most powerful assets is its ability to connect people. Learning becomes more meaningful when it's done in a community setting, where students can exchange ideas, ask questions, and receive feedback.

Online study groups, academic forums, and creator-led communities have emerged across platforms like Reddit, Discord, and even YouTube Shorts.

- Students use Reddit's r/AskScience for complex scientific questions.
- YouTube creators host live Q&A sessions about exam prep and career advice.
- Discord servers allow students to form virtual study groups.

5. Building a Learning Habit – From Passive to Active

The ultimate key to turning social media into a tool for learning is building a structured, intentional habit.

- Set time limits – Allocate specific periods for learning-based content.
- Track your progress – Keep a journal of key insights from educational content.
- Engage with content – Comment, ask questions, and start conversations to deepen understanding.

Practical Tips – How to Use Social Media Strategically

Understanding the psychological and cognitive impact of social media is only the first step. The real challenge lies in applying that knowledge to develop healthier, more intentional social media habits. Social media is designed to maximize engagement and screen time, but with the right strategies, you can turn it into a powerful tool for learning and growth rather than a source of distraction and anxiety.

1. Set Time Limits – Control Your Consumption

Social media platforms are designed to keep you engaged for as long as possible. Features like infinite scrolling and autoplay are built to bypass your brain's natural stop signals, encouraging prolonged use.

Tools to Use:

- StayFocusd – A Chrome extension that limits time spent on specific websites.
- Forest – A gamified app that helps you stay off your phone by "planting a tree" when you avoid distractions.
- Screen Time (iOS) / Digital Wellbeing (Android) – Built-in features that allow you to monitor and limit daily app usage.

2. Curate Your Feed – Follow High-Value Accounts

Algorithms feed you more of what you engage with. If you like, comment on, and share prank videos or influencer drama, the algorithm will flood your feed with similar content. But if you engage with educational, motivational, and skill-building content, the algorithm will adjust to serve you more of that.

To curate your feed:

- Unfollow accounts that create stress or trigger comparison.

- Follow accounts that provide educational value or inspiration.
- Engage with positive, meaningful content to help the algorithm adjust.

3. Use Social Media as a Research Tool

Social media isn't just for entertainment—it's also a powerful research and learning tool. Platforms like YouTube and Instagram host a wealth of educational content created by experts and educators.

How to Use Social Media for Research:

- Follow subject-specific hashtags (e.g., #PhysicsExplained, #FinancialLiteracy).
- Join educational forums and discussion groups.
- Watch expert-led live sessions and Q&A events.

4. Engage Actively – Create Instead of Just Consuming

One of the best ways to solidify knowledge is to teach it to others. Social media provides an ideal platform for this. Creating content not only reinforces your learning but also builds confidence and communication skills.

Ways to Create Content:

- Start a YouTube channel explaining math concepts.
- Create an Instagram account to share book summaries.
- Post Reels breaking down historical events or science facts.

5. Balance Social Media with Offline Learning

While social media can enhance learning, it's not a replacement for deeper engagement with books, long-form articles, and real-world experiences. Social media works best as a supplement—not a substitute—for traditional learning methods.

Tips for Finding Balance:

- Schedule "phone-free" study blocks to focus on deep work.
- Use social media for quick reference or reinforcement, not primary learning.
- Keep a balance between digital and physical learning materials.

The journey from passive scrolling to intentional engagement with social media is not an abstract concept—it's a shift that many students have successfully made. The key to transforming social media from a source of distraction into a tool for growth lies in understanding its mechanisms, setting clear boundaries, and actively curating the content you engage with.

Key Principles for Healthy Social Media Use:

- Mindful Consumption – Be aware of why you're using social media and how it makes you feel.
- Curated Engagement – Follow accounts that educate, motivate, or inspire you.
- Active Participation – Engage with content by commenting, sharing, and creating.

- Balanced Usage – Pair short-form content with deeper engagement through books and research.
- Set Boundaries – Use time limits and app restrictions to prevent overuse.

"We scroll for hours, looking for something to fill the emptiness we refuse to confront."

CHAPTER 10

The Role of Parents – More Than Just Providers

"Parents are the first teachers and the strongest role models. Their words become their child's inner voice, and their actions shape the foundation of their child's future."

Being a parent is one of the most challenging and rewarding roles in life. Every parent wants the best for their child, but sometimes, in the rush to provide food, clothing, and education, the deeper role of parenting gets overlooked. Parenting is not just about ensuring that a child has books and school fees paid—it's about guiding them, supporting them emotionally, and shaping their mindset toward learning and life.

A child's first teacher is their parent. Long before they step into a classroom, children learn by watching and listening to their parents. They pick up habits, values, and attitudes towards learning at home. If a parent treats education as just a responsibility, a child will see it as a burden. But if a parent fosters curiosity, encourages exploration, and shows excitement about learning, the child will naturally develop a love for knowledge.

How Parents Shape a Child's Mindset

Children absorb everything around them—what parents say, how they react to challenges, and how they handle failure. A parent who constantly encourages effort over results teaches a child the importance of persistence. On the other hand, a child who is only rewarded for high grades might grow up fearing failure rather than embracing learning.

It is crucial for parents to create an environment where learning is not just about marks but about understanding and growth. Instead of asking, 'How many marks did you get?' try asking, 'What did you learn today?' This simple change in conversation shifts the focus from performance to progress.

The Power of Encouragement and Emotional Support

Children, like all of us, experience doubts and struggles. A single word of encouragement from a parent can make all the difference. When a child feels supported, they become more confident in taking on challenges. Encouragement doesn't mean praising blindly—it means acknowledging effort, guiding when needed, and reassuring them that mistakes are part of the journey.

Parents play a significant role in shaping their child's resilience. When children face setbacks, they look to their parents for cues on how to react. If parents treat failure as a learning opportunity, children will develop the strength to keep going despite difficulties. But if failure is met with harsh criticism, children may grow fearful of taking risks, limiting their growth.

Creating a Positive Learning Environment at Home

A child's attitude toward learning is shaped not just in school but also at home. The home environment plays a crucial role in determining whether a child sees learning as an enjoyable process or as a stressful burden. Parents who create a positive and encouraging atmosphere at home help their children develop curiosity and confidence in learning.

One of the simplest ways to encourage learning is by making knowledge a part of daily life. Instead of treating education as something that only happens in school, parents can integrate learning into everyday activities. Reading together, discussing interesting topics at the dinner table, and encouraging children to explore their interests outside of textbooks all contribute to a richer learning experience.

The Role of Communication in Strengthening Parent-Child Relationships

Good communication between parents and children is essential for building trust and emotional security. A child who feels heard and understood is more likely to express their thoughts, share their struggles, and seek guidance when needed. Unfortunately, in many households, conversations about school are limited to asking about grades and homework. While academics are important, it's equally crucial to talk about feelings, interests, and personal growth.

Instead of only asking, 'Did you finish your homework?' try asking, 'What was the most interesting thing you learned today?' This shift in conversation shows that education is not just about completing tasks but about discovering new ideas. Similarly, when children face difficulties, parents should listen patiently rather than immediately offering solutions. Sometimes, a child just needs to be heard and reassured that challenges are a normal part of learning.

Why Comparing Children with Others is Harmful

One of the most common yet damaging mistakes parents make is comparing their children with others. Statements like, 'Look at how well your cousin studies' or 'Your friend got better marks than you' may seem harmless, but they can deeply affect a child's self-esteem and motivation. Every child is unique, with their own strengths, interests, and pace of learning. Comparing them to others creates unnecessary pressure and can lead to self-doubt.

Instead of focusing on how a child performs in relation to others, parents should encourage self-improvement. The only real competition a child should have is with themselves—becoming better than they were yesterday. When parents celebrate effort, progress, and resilience instead of just results, children grow with confidence and a positive attitude toward learning.

Another common scenes after an exam is parents anxiously scanning their child's question paper, trying to figure out what went right and what went wrong. Instead of asking their child how they felt during the exam or whether they were comfortable with the questions, many parents jump straight into evaluating the answers. This often leads to immediate scolding, rebuking, or even shouting at the child for their mistakes.

For a child who is already nervous about their performance, such behavior feels like an emotional blow. The child may have put in sincere efforts, but rather than receiving appreciation for their hard work, they are made to feel like a failure. This constant criticism creates a deep-rooted fear of exams and an unhealthy obsession with marks. The focus shifts from learning and understanding to simply securing high scores to avoid parental anger. Over time, this can damage the child's self-esteem and lead to exam anxiety, reduced motivation, and even resentment towards their parents.

Another harmful habit seen in many households is the tendency of parents to compare their child's marks or percentage with that of their classmates, neighbors, or even cousins. Phrases like "Your cousin scored 95%, why can't you?" or "Look at Sharma ji's son, always topping the class" are unfortunately common in many homes.

Such comparisons are extremely damaging. Every child is unique, with different strengths, interests, and learning speeds. Comparing them to others ignores this individuality and sends a message that their worth is measured only by their marks, not their efforts, talents, or personal growth. This can create feelings of inferiority, jealousy, and frustration in children. They may even develop a belief that no matter how hard they try, they will never be "good enough" for their parents.

Parents need to remember that their role is to guide, support, and nurture their child — not to act as examiners or critics. After an exam, the most important thing they can do is to listen to their child's experience, praise their efforts, and gently discuss areas where they can improve.

Instead of comparisons, parents should encourage children to compete with themselves — to aim for personal growth rather than trying to outscore someone else. By creating a safe, supportive environment at home, parents can help children develop a healthy attitude towards both success and failure. This not only improves academic performance but also builds emotional resilience, confidence, and a lifelong love for learning.

Teaching Children Self-Discipline and Responsibility

One of the most valuable lessons parents can teach their children is how to take responsibility for their own actions, especially in their education. Success in learning does not come from external pressure alone—it comes from a student's own motivation, self-discipline, and ability to manage time effectively. Parents play a crucial role in helping their children develop these qualities.

Encouraging children to take ownership of their learning means allowing them to make decisions and experience the consequences. For example, instead of forcing a child to complete homework, parents can guide them in setting their own study schedule. If a child forgets an assignment, rather than immediately solving the problem for them, parents can help them reflect on how to improve their time management. The goal is to help children become independent learners who can handle responsibilities on their own.

Balancing Encouragement and Pressure

Every parent wants their child to do well, but there is a fine line between encouragement and pressure. When parents constantly push for high performance without considering the child's individual strengths and struggles, it can lead to stress and anxiety. On the other hand, when parents provide encouragement and celebrate effort rather than just results, children feel motivated to improve.

Instead of saying, 'You must get the highest marks,' a better approach is to say, 'Give your best effort and keep improving.' This removes the fear of failure and allows children to focus on learning rather than just competing. Parents should set expectations that are challenging yet realistic, ensuring that their child feels supported rather than burdened.

Being Supportive Without Being Controlling

Parental involvement in a child's education is essential, but it should be supportive, not controlling. Some parents, in their desire to see their child succeed, end up making all decisions for them—choosing their subjects, planning their schedule, and even deciding their future career paths. While guidance is important, children also need the space to explore their own interests and make choices.

A healthy balance is when parents provide support, guidance, and encouragement while allowing their children to take responsibility for their learning. This builds confidence and decision-making skills, preparing them not just for academic success, but for life beyond school as well.

Setting a Good Example: Children Learn by Watching

Children learn more from what they see than from what they are told. Parents are their child's first role models, and the behaviors, attitudes, and habits they display have a lasting impact. If a parent values education, curiosity, and hard work, the child is more likely to adopt those values as well. On the other hand, if a child sees their parents avoiding challenges or not prioritizing learning, they might develop the same mindset.

One of the best ways parents can encourage learning is by demonstrating it themselves. Reading books, discussing ideas, and showing an interest in gaining new knowledge sends a powerful message to children—that learning is a lifelong journey, not just something that happens in school.

Creating a Culture of Lifelong Learning at Home

A home that encourages curiosity and exploration helps children develop a natural love for learning. Parents can create this environment by making learning enjoyable rather than a duty. Simple activities like solving puzzles together, watching educational documentaries, and having discussions about current events can spark curiosity and critical thinking.

Encouraging children to ask questions—and taking the time to answer them—helps develop their problem-solving abilities. Instead of saying, 'Because I said so,' parents can encourage deeper thinking by responding with, 'That's an interesting question, let's find out together.' This approach not only builds knowledge but also strengthens the parent-child bond.

Emotional Support: As Important as Academic Support

While academic success is important, emotional well-being is just as crucial. Many students experience stress, anxiety, and self-doubt, and a supportive home environment can make all the difference. Parents who listen without judgment, offer reassurance during difficult times, and celebrate small achievements help their children develop confidence and resilience.

Sometimes, a child simply needs to hear, 'I believe in you.' Knowing that their parents support them unconditionally gives children the courage to take on challenges, face failures, and keep striving to do better. The strongest students are not just those with good grades, but those who feel secure, valued, and capable of achieving their goals.

The Psychology of Raising a Child: How Parents Shape Learning

Parenting is not just about providing for a child's physical needs—it is about shaping their thoughts, emotions, and learning behaviors. Psychology plays a crucial role in understanding how children develop, how they absorb knowledge, and how they respond to their surroundings. By understanding some fundamental psychological theories, parents can support their children in ways that encourage both academic success and personal growth.

Key Psychological Theories Related to Child Development

Several psychological theories explain how children learn and grow. Let's explore a few that are particularly relevant for parents:

Piaget's Theory of Cognitive Development

Jean Piaget, a Swiss psychologist, explained that children go through different stages of thinking as they grow. Young children learn through hands-on experiences and observation. As they get older, they start thinking more logically and abstractly. Parents who provide age-appropriate challenges and encourage problem-solving help their children develop stronger cognitive skills.

Vygotsky's Theory of Social Learning

Lev Vygotsky emphasized that learning happens through social interaction. When parents engage in discussions, answer questions, and guide their children through challenges, they play a critical role in shaping intelligence. He introduced the concept of the 'Zone of Proximal Development'—the idea that children learn best when they are guided slightly beyond their current abilities.

Skinner's Theory of Reinforcement

B.F. Skinner introduced the idea that behaviors are learned through rewards and consequences. When parents praise effort rather than just results, children are more likely to develop a love for learning. A simple 'I'm proud of you for trying' can be more powerful than rewarding only high grades.

Attachment Theory

John Bowlby's attachment theory suggests that a strong emotional bond with parents helps children feel secure and confident. A child who feels emotionally supported is more likely to take risks, explore, and engage in learning without fear of failure.

How Understanding Psychology Helps Parents Support Learning

By applying these psychological principles, parents can create a learning environment that fosters curiosity, confidence, and resilience. For example, instead of forcing a child to memorize facts, parents can use Vygotsky's approach by engaging in discussions and interactive learning. Instead of punishing mistakes, parents can use reinforcement techniques to encourage persistence.

Understanding child psychology allows parents to respond to their children's needs in a way that builds motivation rather than fear. When children feel supported, they are more likely to develop a love for learning that lasts a lifetime.

Parenting: A Continuous Journey, Not Just a Responsibility

As we reach the end of this chapter, one thing becomes clear—parenting is not just about providing education, food, and shelter. It is a continuous journey of guidance, patience, and love. The role of parents in a child's education extends far beyond school; it is about shaping their thoughts, character, and future.

Every child is different, and there is no single formula for perfect parenting. Some children need more encouragement, while others need more independence. Some learn best through structured study, while others thrive through exploration and creativity. The best thing a parent can do is to truly understand their child—their strengths, their struggles, and their dreams.

"Children learn more from what you are than what you teach."

– W.E.B. DuBois

Shaping Not Just Education, but Character and Future

A child's success is not just measured by grades or career achievements—it is also reflected in their kindness, resilience, and ability to face challenges. Education is important, but it is equally important to teach values like honesty, empathy, and perseverance. The lessons parents teach at home—whether through words or actions—become the foundation upon which a child builds their life.

As parents, the most powerful tool you have is your example. Show your children that learning is not just something they do for exams—it is a lifelong journey. Encourage them to ask questions, to think critically, and to explore new ideas. Support their dreams, and when they fail, remind them that failure is just another step toward growth.

A Final Message to Parents

Parenting is not always easy. There will be moments of frustration, doubt, and exhaustion. But remember, the effort you put into guiding your child today will shape the person they become tomorrow. Your words, your encouragement, and your belief in them will stay with them for life.

So be patient, be supportive, and most of all, be present. A child who knows they are loved, supported, and encouraged will have the confidence to take on the world. Education is not just about what happens in school—it is about what happens in the home, in conversations, in daily experiences, and in the small moments that build a lifetime.

Your role as a parent is one of the most important in the world. Embrace it with love, and you will not just raise a well-educated child—you will raise a thoughtful, capable, and compassionate human being.

CHAPTER 11

How Exams Are Conducted and How They Should Be Improved

Examinations have long been the primary way to assess students' knowledge and skills. In most schools and colleges, students take periodic tests, term exams, and final board exams to evaluate their learning progress. These exams are typically written tests that measure how well students remember facts, solve problems, and apply concepts within a limited time.

The idea behind exams is simple—to test what students have learned and to help teachers assess their understanding. However, over time, exams have become more about scoring high marks than about truly measuring knowledge. Many students focus on memorizing textbooks instead of actually understanding the subjects, and this has led to a system where grades are valued more than learning.

Why Exams Are Important

Exams play an important role in education. They provide structure, ensure students stay on track, and help identify areas where improvement is needed. A well-designed exam encourages students to study consistently and apply their knowledge in a structured manner. It also helps teachers and schools measure the effectiveness of their teaching methods.

However, the way exams are conducted today has several flaws. Many tests focus too much on rote memorization instead of real understanding. Students who can memorize well often score higher, even if they do not fully grasp the concepts. On the other hand, students who understand the subject but struggle with time-bound written tests may receive lower scores, creating an unfair assessment system.

The Pressure of Exams and Its Consequences

One of the biggest issues with the current exam system is the immense pressure it puts on students. From a young age, students are told that their future depends on their exam scores. This leads to extreme stress, anxiety, and even fear of failure. Instead of enjoying the process of learning, many students see education as a burden.

The fear of exams has even led to unhealthy practices such as last-minute cramming, cheating, and rote learning. Many students study just to pass exams rather than to gain knowledge. The focus shifts from learning and creativity to achieving the highest possible marks, often at the cost of mental well-being.

Clearly, while exams are important, the way they are conducted needs improvement. A good examination system should test real understanding, encourage curiosity, and support the overall development of students—not just rank them based on numbers.

The Flaws in the Current Examination System

While exams are meant to assess learning, the current system often measures memory rather than understanding. Many exams focus on recalling facts rather than testing how well a student can apply knowledge. This encourages rote memorization, where students memorize textbook definitions without truly grasping the meaning.

For example, a student might be able to write a perfect definition of a scientific concept but may not be able to explain how it works in real life. This gap between memorization and understanding is a major flaw in traditional exams. Instead of assessing true learning, exams often reward those who can memorize the most information within a short period.

Exams and Unnecessary Competition

Another issue with the examination system is the excessive competition it creates. Students are ranked based on their marks, which leads to constant comparison. Instead of focusing on personal improvement, many students feel pressured to outperform their peers. This competition can create anxiety and reduce the joy of learning.

Collaboration is an essential skill in the real world, yet exams rarely encourage teamwork. In most cases, students are expected to work alone, without discussion or problem-solving with others. In contrast, many careers require teamwork, communication, and critical thinking—skills that are not tested in traditional exams.

Developing a Healthier Approach to Exams

Students can develop a better approach to exams by shifting their mindset from marks to mastery. Instead of studying just to pass a test, they should focus on truly understanding concepts. Studying with curiosity, asking questions, and relating topics to real life can make learning more meaningful.

Managing stress is also important. Exams should be seen as an opportunity to learn and improve, not as a life-or-death situation. Good time management, regular revision, and taking breaks while studying can help reduce anxiety. Parents and teachers should also play a role in encouraging students to see education as a journey, not just a race for high marks.

If exams are to be truly effective, they should test creativity, critical thinking, and real-world application—not just memory. A student's ability to solve problems and think independently is far more valuable than their ability to memorize pages of information.

Global Best Practices in Conducting Examinations

Across the world, different countries have developed innovative examination methods to better assess student learning. Some of the best education systems move away from the idea of testing memory and instead emphasize creativity, problem-solving, and practical applications of knowledge. Finland, for instance, has transformed its examination approach by eliminating high-pressure tests in favor of continuous assessments, project-based learning, and practical assignments. The Finnish model ensures that students grasp concepts deeply, rather than memorizing information only to forget it after exams.

Similarly, Japan has integrated moral education and real-world applications into its evaluation system. While university entrance exams in Japan are highly competitive, school-level assessments focus on group activities, discussions, and problem-solving exercises that develop students' teamwork and analytical skills. Instead of placing the burden entirely on individual performance, the Japanese system encourages collaboration and critical thinking.

Germany, on the other hand, follows a dual-track education model where students can choose between academic and vocational training. Examinations in Germany often include practical tests, hands-on projects, and real-life applications, preparing students for both higher education and skilled professions. This system ensures that students are not just theoretically knowledgeable but also ready to tackle real-world challenges.

How India Can Improve Its Examination System

India's education system places a heavy emphasis on theoretical knowledge, leading many students to rely on rote memorization. By learning from global best practices, India can shift towards a more holistic approach to evaluation. A reduction in high-stakes examinations can be replaced with a system that evaluates students through continuous assessment, project-based assignments, and real-world applications.

To ensure exams test real learning, India could incorporate more open-ended questions that encourage critical thinking, practical assessments that measure problem-solving abilities, and a stronger focus on creativity rather than memorization. Schools should also allow for more interdisciplinary learning, where students can apply knowledge from multiple subjects to solve real-life problems. A less stressful examination system that prioritizes understanding over grades can create a more capable and confident generation of learners.

A Look at Ancient and Medieval Examination Systems

Examinations have been a part of education for centuries, but their purpose and methods have evolved over time. Ancient Indian education, especially in the Gurukul system, emphasized personalized learning. Students lived with their teachers and were evaluated through debates, oral discussions, and practical applications rather than written exams. The focus was on developing wisdom, ethical values, and the ability to apply knowledge in everyday life.

In ancient China, one of the earliest standardized examination systems was introduced for selecting government officials. The Imperial Civil Service Examinations were highly rigorous, testing candidates on literature, philosophy, and administrative skills. While this ensured that governance was led by knowledgeable individuals, it also created immense pressure and was criticized for favoring rote learning over practical ability.

During medieval times in Europe, the apprenticeship model was a common method of education. Instead of traditional exams, students learned directly under a master in their chosen field. Their progress was evaluated based on their ability to demonstrate skills rather than pass written tests. This method ensured that students acquired hands-on experience and real-world knowledge, something that modern examination systems often lack.

Lessons from the Past for Today's Education

By examining both historical and modern education systems, it is clear that assessments should go beyond mere memorization. The best examination systems focus on real-world applications, creativity, and problem-solving. India has the opportunity to blend the strengths of ancient personalized learning with modern assessment techniques used in global education models.

Moving forward, examinations should be designed to assess how well students can apply their knowledge, think critically, and solve real-life problems. A well-structured education system that prioritizes understanding over grades will help build a generation of innovative thinkers and lifelong learners.

Alternative Assessment Methods for a Better Learning Experience

Traditional exams are not the only way to evaluate a student's knowledge and skills. Many progressive education systems have started adopting alternative assessment methods that focus on creativity, critical thinking, and real-world applications. Instead of relying solely on written tests, modern education should encourage students to express their understanding in diverse ways.

One effective approach is project-based assessment, where students are required to complete research projects, experiments, or presentations on real-world topics. This method not only tests their understanding of concepts but also enhances problem-solving, teamwork, and communication skills. Such assessments prepare students for future careers, where the ability to apply knowledge is more important than merely recalling facts.

The Role of Technology in Modernizing Exams

Technology has transformed almost every aspect of life, and education is no exception. With advancements in artificial intelligence and adaptive learning, exams can be personalized to suit different learning paces. AI-powered assessment tools can analyze student performance and provide customized feedback, helping learners improve in specific areas rather than just assigning grades.

Online assessments are another way technology is revolutionizing exams. Digital platforms can create interactive exams with videos, simulations, and real-time problem-solving tasks, making the assessment process more engaging and relevant. Unlike traditional exams, which often encourage rote memorization, technology-driven assessments can evaluate higher-order thinking skills.

The Importance of Open-Book and Application-Based Exams

In many parts of the world, open-book exams are gaining popularity as an alternative to closed-book memory-based tests. These exams do not focus on how much information a student can remember but rather on how well they can apply knowledge to solve problems. In open-book exams, students are allowed to use reference materials, encouraging them to analyze, interpret, and think critically rather than just recall facts.

Additionally, oral exams, group discussions, and case study-based assessments help students articulate their ideas and develop reasoning skills. A well-rounded evaluation system should include a mix of written, verbal, and practical assessments to ensure students are truly prepared for the real-world challenges they will face after their education.

By integrating alternative assessment methods, technology-driven exams, and application-based evaluations, education systems can create a more balanced and effective approach to learning. The goal should not be to test how well students memorize but to evaluate how well they can think, analyze, and solve real-world problems.

The Future of Exams: Shifting Toward Meaningful Assessments

Examinations are a fundamental part of education, but they should evolve to truly reflect a student's learning journey. The purpose of assessment should not be to create unnecessary pressure or rank students against one another but to guide them toward deeper understanding and real-world application of knowledge. A meaningful examination system should focus on evaluating creativity, problem-solving, and the ability to think critically rather than just measuring memory.

The current education system needs to find a balance between structured assessments and holistic learning. Exams should be designed to assess not just academic performance but also emotional intelligence, leadership skills, and adaptability. A student's worth should not be determined by a single exam but by their continuous growth, curiosity, and contributions to society.

Balancing Assessment and Holistic Education

A well-rounded education system values both academic knowledge and life skills. Instead of relying solely on timed tests, evaluations should include experiential learning, project-based assessments, and peer collaborations. Schools and universities should emphasize the importance of applying knowledge rather than just acquiring it.

A truly effective examination system will allow students to explore their interests, develop critical thinking, and prepare for future challenges with confidence. Exams should not be seen as obstacles but as tools for reflection, improvement, and real-world readiness.

A Call for Change: Encouraging a New Perspective on Examinations

As students, teachers, and policymakers, we must rethink the way we approach exams. Change will not happen overnight, but every small step toward reforming assessments will lead to a better future for learners. The education system must embrace innovation, adopt modern evaluation techniques, and prioritize the overall development of students.

Exams should be a stepping stone to learning, not a roadblock. The goal should be to create lifelong learners who are curious, resilient, and capable of adapting to an ever-changing world. If we can shift our focus from scoring marks to gaining knowledge, we will build a generation of thinkers, leaders, and innovators who are ready to shape the future.

"An exam can measure answers, but not abilities. True success lies not in never falling, but in rising every time you fall."

CHAPTER 12

A Lifelong Learner

Education does not stop when we finish school or college. While formal education lays the foundation for knowledge, there are many other forms of learning that shape individuals, communities, and even entire nations. True education is about developing the skills, values, and understanding necessary to lead a fulfilling life and contribute meaningfully to society.

For a nation to grow, its people must continue learning beyond textbooks and classrooms. Individuals who seek knowledge in various fields become innovators, responsible citizens, and leaders who drive progress. Let's explore the essential types of education that help us grow as individuals and as a nation.

Financial Education

Understanding how to manage money is crucial for both individuals and the nation. Financial education teaches people about saving, investing, budgeting, and financial independence. A financially literate population leads to stronger economies, lower debt, and a higher standard of living. Despite its importance, financial literacy is often missing from formal education systems, leaving many people unprepared for real-life financial decisions.

Health and Nutrition Education

Good health is the foundation of a productive life. Education on physical and mental well-being helps individuals make informed choices about diet, exercise, mental health, and hygiene. A healthy population leads to a more efficient workforce, lower healthcare costs, and a higher quality of life. Schools should incorporate health and nutrition education to ensure that young people develop lifelong habits that promote wellness.

Civic Education

A strong nation is built on responsible and informed citizens. Civic education teaches people about their rights, duties, and how governments function. It empowers individuals to participate in democratic processes, make informed decisions, and work towards the betterment of society. Without civic awareness, people may not exercise their rights or take responsibility for social progress.

Entrepreneurial and Skill-Based Education

A nation thrives when its people are not just job seekers but also job creators. Entrepreneurial education encourages innovation, problem-solving, and risk-taking. Skill-based learning, including technical and vocational training, ensures that individuals are equipped for real-world challenges. Instead of relying solely on degrees, students should also gain practical skills that enhance their career opportunities and contribute to economic growth.

Environmental Education

A sustainable future requires awareness about environmental issues. Education on climate change, conservation, and sustainability teaches people how to make responsible choices that protect the planet. Governments, businesses, and individuals all have a role to play in preserving natural resources for future generations.

Technological and Digital Literacy

In the digital age, understanding technology is no longer optional—it is a necessity. Digital literacy enables individuals to use technology responsibly, stay safe online, and leverage digital tools for learning and career growth. With advancements in artificial intelligence and automation, continuous learning in technology will be essential to stay relevant in the future job market.

As we can see, learning goes far beyond textbooks and exams. The more we educate ourselves in these diverse fields, the better prepared we are to lead successful lives and contribute to the progress of our nation. However, simply knowing what to learn is not enough. We must also develop the mindset of a lifelong learner.

What It Means to Be a Lifelong Learner

Learning is not confined to childhood or the years spent in formal education. Being a lifelong learner means having the curiosity, openness, and willingness to keep acquiring knowledge and skills throughout life. It is about constantly seeking improvement, adapting to change, and embracing new ideas. In a rapidly evolving world, those who continue to learn remain adaptable, innovative, and prepared for the future.

A lifelong learner does not wait for opportunities to learn—they create them. Whether it is reading books, learning new skills, taking online courses, or engaging in discussions, they make learning a habit. This mindset helps individuals stay relevant in their careers, grow personally, and contribute positively to society.

The Mindset of Continuous Growth and Curiosity

Lifelong learners possess a growth mindset—the belief that intelligence and abilities are not fixed but can be developed with effort and persistence. They are not afraid of making mistakes because they see failures as learning opportunities. They ask questions, explore different perspectives, and remain open to new experiences.

Curiosity is a key trait of lifelong learners. They do not just seek answers; they question the world around them. Instead of accepting information at face value, they investigate deeper, analyze different viewpoints, and make informed decisions. Whether it is understanding new technology, exploring different cultures, or gaining wisdom from history, lifelong learners keep their minds active and engaged.

How Lifelong Learning Benefits Personal Success and National Progress

On a personal level, lifelong learning enhances confidence, career opportunities, and problem-solving abilities. Those who keep learning can adapt to new job roles, develop expertise in multiple fields, and build resilience in an ever-changing world. Instead of feeling stuck, they see every challenge as an opportunity to grow.

On a larger scale, when a nation encourages lifelong learning, it leads to innovation, economic growth, and social progress. Countries that invest in continuous education—whether through skill development programs, research initiatives, or digital learning platforms—create a workforce that is capable, creative, and competitive. A well-educated population leads to better decision-making, stronger communities, and a more prosperous society.

The world is evolving at an unprecedented pace, and those who stop learning risk being left behind. Whether young or old, rich or poor, formal degree holders or self-taught individuals—everyone has the capacity to continue learning.

How to Develop the Habit of Lifelong Learning

Lifelong learning is not just about formal education—it is about creating a habit of continuous self-improvement. To truly become a lifelong learner, one must make learning an intentional and natural part of everyday life. The good news is that anyone can develop this habit, regardless of age, background, or profession.

The key to lifelong learning is to stay curious. Instead of thinking of learning as a task, see it as an opportunity to explore new ideas, gain different perspectives, and improve skills that will help in both personal and professional life. A lifelong learner embraces challenges, seeks feedback, and is always open to growth.

Practical Ways to Stay Curious and Continuously Improve

There are many ways to integrate learning into daily life. Here are some practical methods that help maintain curiosity and continuous improvement:

1. Read Regularly: Books, articles, and research papers expose us to new ideas, historical knowledge, and industry trends. Reading expands the mind and improves comprehension, vocabulary, and analytical thinking.
2. Learn by Doing: Hands-on experience is one of the most effective ways to learn. Whether it's experimenting with a new skill, starting a personal project, or working on a real-world problem, practical application deepens understanding.

3. Surround Yourself with Knowledgeable People: Engaging in conversations with experts, mentors, or even peers who have diverse knowledge helps expand one's thinking. Discussions and debates encourage critical thinking and introduce new perspectives.

4. Ask Questions and Stay Curious: The best learners never stop asking 'Why?' and 'How?'. Instead of accepting things as they are, they challenge themselves to understand the deeper reasons behind concepts and ideas.

Different Learning Methods: Finding What Works Best

Every individual has a unique way of learning. Some people absorb knowledge best through reading, while others prefer hands-on practice. Here are three effective learning methods:

1. Learning Through Reading: Books and articles provide structured knowledge on a wide range of subjects. Reading autobiographies, case studies, and research reports can give valuable insights and lessons from experts.

2. Learning Through Experience: Practical exposure, whether through internships, travel, or real-world projects, allows individuals to apply concepts to real situations. Experience-based learning is especially useful in skill-based professions and entrepreneurial ventures.

3. Learning Through Mentorship: Learning from experienced mentors can accelerate growth. Mentors provide guidance, share their experiences, and help learners avoid common mistakes.

By combining these learning methods, individuals can continuously grow in their personal and professional lives. The goal is not just to acquire knowledge but to develop the ability to adapt, innovate, and contribute to society.

What Great Minds Say About Lifelong Learning

Throughout history, some of the world's greatest minds have spoken about the importance of continuous learning. Their words remind us that true wisdom comes not from knowing everything, but from always seeking to know more.

Albert Einstein once said, 'Intellectual growth should commence at birth and cease only at death.' His words remind us that the quest for knowledge should never end. No matter how much we achieve, there is always something new to explore, understand, and master.

Leonardo da Vinci, the great Renaissance thinker, believed that 'Learning never exhausts the mind.' Unlike physical labor that tires the body, knowledge only expands our horizons. The more we learn, the more doors we open for innovation and creativity.

The famous philosopher Socrates once said, 'I am the wisest man alive, for I know one thing, and that is that

I know nothing.' This simple yet profound thought shows that wisdom is not about having all the answers, but about recognizing that there is always more to learn.

Even in modern times, Bill Gates, one of the most influential figures in technology, has emphasized the power of reading and self-education. He once said, 'I never stopped learning. Every book I read teaches me something new, and every mistake I make is an opportunity to improve.'

These words of wisdom remind us that learning is not just a phase of life—it is the essence of life itself. Whether it is through books, experiences, or personal reflection, we must always remain students of the world.

In the final section, we will discuss how to apply lifelong learning in everyday life and how to make it a guiding principle for personal and professional success.

The Journey of Learning: A Never-Ending Path

Throughout this book, we have explored the many dimensions of learning—what education truly means, how it shapes individuals and societies, and how we can improve it to create a better future. We have looked at the roles of schools, teachers, students, and parents, and we have understood that learning goes beyond textbooks and exams. True education is about growth, curiosity, and the continuous pursuit of wisdom.

We have discussed how moral education builds character, how emotional intelligence strengthens relationships, and how skill-based learning prepares us for real-world challenges. We have explored how technology, co-curricular activities, and lifelong curiosity contribute to a fulfilling and meaningful life. But above all, we have discovered one fundamental truth—learning never ends.

Education is the Key to Personal and National Growth

A nation's progress is determined not by its wealth or military strength but by the education of its people. When individuals commit to continuous learning, they innovate, inspire, and lead. They solve problems, create opportunities, and shape a society that values knowledge, wisdom, and ethical living.

As students, teachers, parents, and citizens, we all have a responsibility—to never stop learning, to keep questioning, and to seek knowledge beyond the classroom. The world is evolving, and only those who embrace learning will adapt, grow, and contribute meaningfully to the future.

Imagine standing at the shore of a vast ocean. The more you learn, the further you step into the waters of knowledge. But no matter how deep you go, the ocean never ends. This is the beauty of learning—it is infinite, and it is for everyone.

Nelson Mandela once said, 'Education is the most powerful weapon which you can use to change the world.' This book is a call to action—to change the world by changing ourselves. To never settle with what we know, but to always seek more. To read, to explore, to fail, to learn from failure, and to rise again with greater wisdom.

If there is one message to take away from this book, it is this: Be a learner for life. The journey of learning is not a race with an end goal—it is a way of living. Let curiosity be your guide, let wisdom be your strength, and let education be the light that leads you forward.

The world belongs to those who keep learning, growing, and evolving. Will you be one of them?

Final Note

As I write this final note, I find myself revisiting the core reason why I started this book — the desire to see our education system truly serve its purpose: to create not just literate individuals, but responsible, ethical, emotionally intelligent, and lifelong learners who actively contribute to society.

Throughout these twelve chapters, I have shared thoughts, ideas, and possible solutions — not as an outsider commenting from a distance, but as a teacher, a learner, and a citizen who deeply cares about the future of our students and our nation.

One thing I want to emphasize, above all, is this: improving education is not just the government's job. It is a responsibility that belongs to each and every one of us. When a student skips class, when a parent ignores their child's curiosity, when a teacher loses faith in their own teaching, or when society views education merely as a means to pass exams — we all contribute to a failing system.

But the opposite is equally true — when a parent reads to their child, when a teacher inspires rather than instructs, when students question fearlessly, and when citizens demand meaningful reforms — we all become part of the solution.

Education cannot thrive in isolation. It needs collaboration between schools and homes, between policies and practice, between society and self. And more importantly, it needs all of us to believe that change is possible.

I am reminded of the powerful words of Dr. A.P.J. Abdul Kalam, who said:

"Let us sacrifice our today so that our children can have a better tomorrow."

But I believe this sacrifice is not about giving up something — it's about actively contributing, in whatever way we can, so that our children inherit not just schools and colleges, but a culture of learning that nurtures their minds and souls.

As I close this book, I humbly invite you — whether you are a teacher, a parent, a student, or simply a concerned citizen — to see yourself as a changemaker in this journey. The government alone cannot build a great education system. Policies may set the direction, but the true spirit of education is shaped in everyday moments — in homes, in classrooms, in communities, and in conversations.

This book is not the final word on education, nor do I claim to have all the answers. But I firmly believe that if we start seeing education as a shared responsibility, if we value curiosity over blind obedience, and if we place ethical, emotional, and moral learning at the heart of all teaching — we can create an education system we are proud to pass on to future generations.

The future of India's education is not written in government files alone. It is written in the hands of every parent, every teacher, every student, and every citizen. And it starts today — with you and me.

Together, let us build the education system our children deserve.